AT HOME WITH
PATRICK
LOSE

COLORFUL
QUILTED
PROJECTS

C&T PUBLISHING

Editor: Annie Nelson
Technical Editors: Sally Loss Lanzarotti and Kathleen Loda
Book Design: John Cram
Front Cover Design: John Cram
Original Watercolor Illustrations: Patrick Lose
Graphic Illustrations: Jay Richards
Photography: Set shots by Perry Struse; all other photos by Steve Struse.
Photo Styling: Patrick Lose and Lenny Houts

Attention Teachers:
C&T Publishing, Inc. encourages you to use this book as a text for teaching. Contact us at 800-284-1114 or www.ctpub.com for more information about the C&T Teachers Program.

Library of Congress Cataloging-in-Publication Data
Lose, Patrick.
At home with Patrick Lose : colorful quilted projects / Patrick Lose.
      p.   cm.
      Includes index.
      ISBN 1-57120-061-4 (pbk.)
        1. Appliqué—Patterns.   2. Patchwork—Patterns.   3. Quilting.
4. Quilts.   I. Title.
TT779.L6696 1999   98-38375
746.46'041—dc21   CIP

Chaco-liner chalk is a product of Clover Needlecraft Inc.
Goody is a registered trademark of Goody Products.
IDentipen is a trademark of Sakura Color Products Corporation of America.
Metosene/Mettler is a brand name of Arova Mettler AG.
Pigma is a registered trademark of Sakura Color Products Corporation of America.
Warm & Natural is a trademark of Warm Products, Inc.
Timeless Treasures is a division of Hi-Fashion Fabrics, Inc.

Published by C&T Publishing, Inc.
P.O. Box 1456
Lafayette, California 94549

Printed in Hong Kong
10   9   8   7   6   5   4   3   2   1

TABLE OF CONTENTS

*This book is dedicated to
the memory of my aunt, Noreen Tiernan.
Her loving encouragement and appreciation for my
work will always be a huge inspiration to me.*

ACKNOWLEDGMENTS

There are several people I wish to thank, and I apologize in advance if I forget anyone in the process. First of all I'm grateful to my partner, Lenny, for putting up with my perfectionism and bringing my ideas to reality with the help of our talented quilting friends, Vivian Irwin, Nan Wakefield, and Shon Jones.

Next, a huge thank you to Todd Hensley and all of the team at C&T Publishing, for so perfectly presenting my ideas to you in this form. I feel very fortunate to have worked with you.

To all of my friends at Hi-Fashion Fabrics/Timeless Treasures™…thank you for your encouragement and support, and for putting my designs on fabric so beautifully.

And, finally, I wish to thank my family and friends, and you, the reader, for your enthusiasm and belief in my work.

INTRODUCTION

This book is a collection of the type of colorful home decorations with which I like to surround myself. It says a lot about me as a designer, and, hopefully, it will inspire you to get busy stitching and quilting.

When designing all of these projects, I knew that I really wanted to emphasize color and the impact that it can have when used effectively. Whether you like making a more traditionally pieced quilt such as *Tulip Garden* (page 18), or you go for a more playful piece like *A Cat For All Seasons* (page 14), I think you will notice, as you look at my designs, that it is probably the coloration that first catches your eye.

There is an infinite number of color combinations I could have used in these projects, and I encourage you to use your own color sense as you create your pieces. I've always been known as a designer that favors a bold approach to color like that used in the quilts *Love and Loyalty* (page 10) and *Woven Rainbow* (page 28). But I have to say that I am just as comfortable using a softer pastel palette as shown in the whimsical baby quilt, *Special Delivery* (page 32), or the earthy, more primitive palette I used in the door topper, *Twilight Blossoms* (page 37). All colors can be exciting; it just depends on how you combine them. You'll know if the mix is right for you when you feel satisfied with it.

You could say that being "At Home with Patrick Lose" happens when you've become comfortable knowing that you can achieve an exciting balance of color, style, and fun!

GENERAL INSTRUCTIONS

GENERAL SEWING

All the projects in this book are sewn using a ¼" seam allowance and are stitched with the fabrics placed right sides together. As tempting as it may be to "jump" right into your project, it is always best to read all of the instructions thoroughly before you begin.

TOOLS

Make sure you have all the necessary tools at hand before you start cutting and stitching up a storm. It's easy to let your excitement for the project at hand get the best of you, and then you're off to the quilt shop to buy more fabric or to hunt for a seam ripper! Following is a list of helpful tools that will make your stitching a lot easier.

Rotary cutter and cutting mat

Transparent acrylic gridded ruler

Scissors
    for cutting fabric
    for cutting paper

Pins

Hand sewing needles

Machine sewing needles, size 80

Pencil

Permanent black marker with an ultra fine tip such as a Pigma Micron® or IDentipen® for marking templates and patterns

Chaco-liner® for marking quilting lines

Seam ripper

Sewing machine capable of doing satin stitch (and blanket/buttonhole stitch if making *A Cat for All Seasons* project)

Walking foot for machine quilting

Darning foot for free-motion quilting

Iron

Template plastic if making *Love and Loyalty* quilt

Light box, if desired

FABRICS

I'm proud to say that all of the fabrics featured in the following projects (with the exception of the white) are of my own design for my *Marble Mania* collection with Timeless Treasures. They are 100% cotton and, of course, come in a wide variety of colors. In the instructions for each project, I've listed a generic color name for the fabrics used. The star, polka dot, and check pattern fabrics featured in the *Pumpkin Party* project (page 41) are from my *More Marble Mania* collection, which is the line of companion prints to the *Marble Mania* collection. See page 102 for ordering information.

I don't pre-wash any of my fabrics for quilting. This is my personal preference based on the fact that I have never had a problem with any of the colors bleeding. If I do wash the finished piece, the minimal shrinkage creates a slightly puckered quilt with a softer look and feel. There are those who always pre-wash, and that is perfectly fine. Just be sure that, if you pre-wash, you do it in warm water to allow the fabric to shrink as much as it is going to. Tumble dry and remove from the dryer when the fabric is still slightly damp. Always iron the fabric before measuring and cutting. Do not use starch on fabrics that will be used for appliqué pieces. It could make fabric difficult to fuse.

It is extremely important to measure and cut your fabrics accurately and to stitch using an exact ¼" seam allowance. I am certain you'll be proud of your finished piece if you follow these simple rules.

APPLIQUÉ

The appliqué projects in this book use a fusible adhesive appliqué method and are outlined using a machine satin stitch. The one exception is the *A Cat for All Seasons* project (page 14), which uses a blanket/button-hole stitch. Should you wish to do hand appliqué (knock yourself out…), you'll need to add seam allowances to the appliqué patterns.

All the patterns in this book for appliqué are printed actual size and are reversed for tracing onto paper-backed fusible adhesive. Be sure to use a lightweight paper-backed fusible adhesive that is suitable for sewing.

Fusible Appliqué

1
Lay your fusible adhesive sheet, paper side up, over the pattern, and trace with a pencil. If the pattern has been dissected to fit on the page, be sure to join the pieces as you trace, by joining the sections indicated on the patterns. Write the pattern name or number on each piece as you trace.

2
Also be sure to trace any appliqué placement lines or stitching detail lines. Do this with a permanent black marker, so you can see these lines

later when you transfer them onto the fabric pieces (see Step 5).

3
Using paper cutting scissors, roughly cut all pieces approximately ¼" outside of the traced pencil lines.

4
Following the project instructions and the instructions provided by the manufacturer for the appropriate heat setting for the brand of fusible adhesive you are using, iron adhesive onto the wrong side of the desired fabric.

5

Cut out the pieces along the pencil lines using a pair of sharp fabric cutting scissors. *Do not remove the paper backing yet.*

6

Transfer any appliqué placement lines (- - -) or detail stitching lines (............) onto the right side of the fabric by placing the piece on a light box or against a window during daylight hours. (It will be easier to see these lines if you have traced the lines with a permanent black marker as explained in Step 2.) Use a pencil to transfer these lines lightly onto the right side of the fabric; the pencil lines will be covered by stitching.

7

When you are ready to position your appliqué, remove the paper backing. Before fusing pieces that "butt up" to one another, overlap them slightly (1/16" or less) so that there are no gaps in between pieces. Position as instructed, and when you are satisfied with the placement, iron it onto the background fabric using the appropriate heat setting that is given by the manufacturer with the fusible adhesive instructions. Fuse one piece at a time. If you would like to reposition a piece after fusing, you can usually do this by warming the piece with an iron and peeling it off. Reposition and fuse.

Satin Stitch

Use a satin stitch around the appliqué after the quilt top, batting, and backing are basted together. To satin stitch around the appliqué, try Metrosene/Mettler® embroidery thread in matching colors (unless otherwise noted), using a fairly narrow zigzag stitch. If you are new to satin stitched appliqué, it is best to practice on a scrap of fabric. Whenever possible, work outward from the center of the quilt. Keep your stitch length as close as possible to completely cover the raw edges.

For a couple of the projects, I have used a permanent black marker to color the pupils of the eyes. To keep the marker from bleeding, it helps to blow on the area as you are marking.

QUILTING

I like to use a single layer of thin cotton batting such as Warm & Natural®. Cut your backing fabric and batting to measure 2" to 3" larger than your quilt top on all sides. (I allow 2" extra on all sides for small projects and 3" extra on all sides for the larger projects.) Sandwich the batting between the top and backing, wrong sides together, and baste through all layers, smoothing the quilt top outward from the center. You can also use safety pins spaced about 4"-6" apart.

All of the quilting in this book was done by machine. I use a walking foot for quilting. For free-motion or stipple quilting, use a darning foot and lower the feed dogs on your machine. That doesn't mean you can't quilt by hand if you'd like; hand quilting would be a beautiful addition to the look of these pieces. You may quilt as desired or refer to the photos and quilting suggestions that are included with each project. A Chaco-liner is great for marking quilting lines if you are not comfortable "eyeballing" them, and the lines can be easily brushed away. When quilting appliqué projects, be sure to break the quilting path over all the appliqué shapes.

BINDING

The instructions for each project give you the amount of binding necessary to finish your quilt project.

1

I like to use 2⅛"-wide strips cut selvage to selvage using a rotary cutter, mat, and a transparent acrylic gridded ruler. These strips will measure about 44" long, after you have straightened your fabric and cut off the selvages.

2

Use diagonal seams to join binding strips. Trim seam allowance and press the seam open. Fold the completed length of binding in half lengthwise with the wrong sides together. Press.

3

Place the folded binding strip on the right side of the quilt top, beginning in the center of one side and aligning the raw edges of the quilt and the binding. Fold over the beginning of the binding about ½". Stitch through all of the layers using a ¼" seam allowance. Stop stitching ¼" from the corner. Backstitch two or more stitches, remove the quilt from the machine, and clip the threads.

4

Fold the binding up and crease the fold with your fingers.

5

Holding the fold in place, fold the binding down and align the raw edges with the next side of the quilt. Start stitching again at the corner, through all layers. Stitch around the quilt, treating each corner as you did the first.

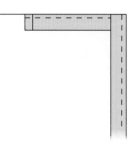

6

When you return to where you started, stitch the binding beyond the fold you made in the strip at the beginning. Backstitch two or more stitches and clip the threads. At this time, cut off the excess batting and backing fabric so that all layers are even.

7

Turn the binding over the quilt edge, aligning the fold of the binding with the machine stitching you just finished. You can pin the binding in place, but I like to use those funny little hair clips that bend/snap closed; they work great and don't get stuck in the carpet. You can find them at most variety or drugstores under the brand name Goody®. Sew the binding in place by hand onto the backing. Make sure you cover the machine stitching. Miter the corners of the backside of the binding also, stitching the fold in place, if necessary.

If you simply refuse to do hand stitching, sew the binding onto the backside of the quilt first. Then, fold it to the front side and pin it in place, mitering your corners. Use monofilament or matching thread and a very narrow width and long zigzag stitch, just catching the edge of the fold of the binding. It's much easier to be sure you're catching the binding this way than if it is on the underside and you're blindly stitching in the ditch. But, you'd have to admit, it would be a lot prettier if you'd just "bite the bullet" and stitch it by hand!

Be sure to display your work of art in a conspicuous place where it is most likely to prompt compliments, but keep in mind that direct sunlight will fade fabric more quickly than you might think.

Love and Loyalty, 1998, 60" x 60"
Designed by Patrick Lose. Quilt top made by Lenny Houts.
Quilted by Vivian Irwin.

LOVE AND LOYALTY

This bold and vibrant piece is the result of my desire to create a quilt that showcased the fabric I designed for my *Marble Mania* collection from Timeless Treasures. Although the majority of the quilt is simply pieced from 6" blocks cut from only four fabrics, the mottling of colors gives the illusion of depth and texture that can only be achieved by using many more fabrics or, as in this case, fabrics that look hand-painted. The crest-like design in the center of the quilt consists of four hearts and four crowns, which I chose to symbolize love and loyalty.

REQUIRED FABRIC AND SUPPLIES

1⅝ yard orange-red

¾ yard green

¾ yard deep purple

4¾ yards gold: ¾ yard for blocks, 4 yards for binding and backing (set aside)

Binding and backing: gold fabric listed above

Thin cotton batting: 66" x 66"

Large sheet of medium-weight template plastic (approximately 18" x 24")

CUTTING BLOCKS

Trace template patterns A, B, C, D, and E, located on pattern pages 49-52, onto template plastic, making sure to write the letter and amount of colors to cut on each template. Note that the ¼" seam allowances have been included.

A quick method to cut these blocks is to cut all the block fabrics into 6½" strips, selvage to selvage, using your rotary cutter, mat, and ruler. Then trace the templates onto the 6½" strips and cut with scissors. **Do not** cut the piece of gold fabric to be used for backing and binding.

ORANGE-RED
From the 6½" strips, cut thirty-two 6½" x 6½" blocks (or use Template A). From the remaining strips, use the templates indicated.

Template B1: cut eight

Template C1: cut four, reverse template and cut four more

Template D1: cut four, reverse template and cut four more

GREEN
From the 6½" strips, cut sixteen 6½" x 6½" blocks. From the strips that remain, use the template indicated.

Template E1: cut four

DEEP PURPLE
From the 6½" strips, cut sixteen 6½" x 6½" blocks. From the strips that remain, use the template indicated.

Template B2: cut eight, reverse template and cut eight more

GOLD
From the 6½" strips, cut eight 6½" x 6½" blocks. From the strips that remain, use the templates indicated.

Template C2: cut four, reverse template and cut four more

Template D2: cut four, reverse template and cut four more

Template E2: cut four

From remaining gold fabric, cut seven 2⅛" x 44" strips selvage to selvage for binding. Cut and piece backing to measure 66" x 66".

ASSEMBLING PIECED BLOCKS

1

Set aside the 6½" × 6½" squares for Block A. Assemble each of Blocks B, C, D, and E as follows:

2

Sew eight B blocks for the upper part of the heart. Press seams toward the orange-red.

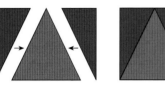

Block B

3

Sew four C blocks for the middle part of the heart. Press seams toward the orange-red.

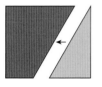

Block C

Repeat, sew four C reverse blocks.

4

Sew four D blocks for the lower part of the heart. Press seams toward the orange-red.

Block D

Repeat, sew four D reverse blocks.

5

Sew two E blocks for the center of the quilt. Press seams toward the green.

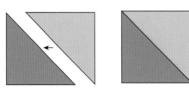

Block E

Repeat, sew two E reverse blocks.

ASSEMBLING THE QUILT TOP

1

Assemble the blocks as indicated, one horizontal row at a time. Press seams in one direction. Press seams in opposite direction in alternating rows.

2

As each row is completed, stitch it to the previous row, matching all seams. Press seams in one direction.

3

Sandwich the batting between the quilt top and backing, wrong sides together, and baste through all layers, smoothing the quilt top outward from the center.

QUILTING

I used a monofilament thread and stitched a lot of straight lines (approximately ½" apart) going in different directions. I did stippling in different sections as well. Refer to General Instructions on page 9 for binding instructions.

A Cat for All Seasons, 1998, 32" x 32"
Designed by Patrick Lose.
Made and quilted by Lenny Houts.

A CAT FOR ALL SEASONS

Here's one for the cat lovers, though these colorful cats are much
too busy enjoying the changing of the seasons to lay curled up in anyone's lap. Spring, summer, autumn, and winter are all depicted here in
buttonhole stitch appliqué and easy piecing. Maybe you'd like to change
the colors of the cats a bit to represent your favorite feline?

REQUIRED FABRIC AND SUPPLIES

Deep green: 1 fat quarter for Spring cat and background for Winter Cat block

Deep yellow: 1 fat quarter for tulip, bird's beak, stars, and background for Summer Cat block

White: 4" x 8" piece of for cats' eyes, moon, and snowflakes

Fuchsia: 14" x 14" piece for background for Spring Cat block and Spring cat's tongue

Black: 8" x 10" piece for cats' pupils, Autumn cat, earmuff band, and sunglasses

Medium blue: 4" x 4" piece for bird and blue beachball sections

Orange-red: 8" x 10" piece for Summer cat

Orange: 4" x 10" piece for Summer cat spots, stripes, nose, ears, and sun

Violet: 14" x 14" piece for background for Autumn Cat block

Light orange: 4" x 6" piece for pumpkin and hat band

Purple: 3" x 3" piece for hat

Avocado green (use the wrong side of the fabric): small scrap for pumpkin stem

Gray: 4" x 7" piece for Autumn cat spots, stripes, nose, and ear

Powder blue: 4" x 7" piece for Winter cat spots, stripes, nose, and ears

Red: 4" x 6" piece for earmuffs and scarf

Lime green: ⅜ piece for sashing; use remaining fabric for Spring cat spots, stripes, nose, ears, tulip stem, and green beachball sections

Medium blue: 1⅜ yards for sashing and backing

Deep blue: ⅜ yard for corner squares and binding: use remaining for Winter cat

Binding: deep blue fabric listed above

Backing: medium blue fabric listed above

Thin cotton batting: 36" x 36"

¾ yard lightweight paper-backed fusible adhesive, suitable for sewing

Thread for piecing

Black machine embroidery thread for buttonhole stitching

Matching thread for quilting

CUTTING FABRICS

Using a rotary cutter, mat, and ruler, cut the following strips selvage to selvage:

LIME GREEN
Four 1" x 44" strips for sashing

MEDIUM BLUE
Eight 1¼" x 44" strips for sashing

One square 36" x 36" for backing

DEEP BLUE
One 2½" x 44" strip. From the 2 ½" strip, cut nine 2½" x 2½" corner squares.

Four 2⅛" x 44" strips for the binding

FUCHSIA, DEEP YELLOW, VIOLET, AND DEEP GREEN
One each 13½" x 13½" square for background blocks

FUSIBLE APPLIQUÉ PREPARATION

All appliqué pattern pieces for this project are on pages 54-58. They are printed actual size and reversed for tracing onto fusible adhesive. Refer to page 7 for instructions on fusible appliqué. Note that you will be using the same pattern for all four cats, but there is a slight variance for the Autumn cat. Also, the mouth on the Spring cat is different. Trace his mouth from the diagram provided with the pattern pieces.

1

Lay the fusible adhesive, paper side up, over each pattern piece and use a pencil to trace onto the paper side. Write the pattern number on each piece as you trace.

2

Be sure to trace any appliqué placement lines or detail stitching lines using a permanent marker.

3

Use paper cutting scissors to roughly cut all the pieces approximately ¼" outside the traced lines.

4

Then, following manufacturers instructions for fusing, fuse the traced pattern onto the wrong side of the fabric indicated by color.

DEEP GREEN, ORANGE-RED, AND DEEP BLUE
1 cat each (C 1)

BLACK
1 cat (C 1); 6 pupils (C 12); 1 sunglasses (C 20); 1 earmuff band (C 33)

LIME GREEN
2 spots (C 2); 7 spots, 1 of each (C 3-9); 9 stripes (C 10); 1 nose (C 13); 2 ears (C 14); 1 tulip stem (C 16); 1 beachball (C 21)

ORANGE
2 spots (C 2); 7 spots, 1 of each (C 3-9); 9 stripes (C 10); 1 nose (C 13); 2 ears (C 14); 1 sun (C 24)

GRAY
2 spots (C 2); 7 spots, 1 of each (C 3-9); 9 stripes (C 10); 1 nose (C 13); 1 ear (C 14)

POWDER BLUE
1 spot (C 2); 1 spot (C-3); 5 spots, 1 of each (C 5-9); 9 stripes (C 10); 1 nose (C 13); 2 ears (C 14)

WHITE
6 eyes (C 11); 1 moon (C 29); 9 snowflakes (C 36)

FUCHSIA
1 tongue (C 15)

DEEP YELLOW
1 tulip (C 17); 1 bird beak (C 19); 1 star (C 30); 1 star (C 31)

MEDIUM BLUE
1 bird (C 18); 1 stripe on ball (C 22); 1 stripe on ball (C 23)

PURPLE
1 hat (C 25)

LIGHT ORANGE
1 hat band (C 26); 1 pumpkin (C 27)

AVOCADO GREEN
1 pumpkin stem (C 28)

RED
1 scarf (C 32); 1 left earmuff (C 34); 1 right earmuff (C 35)

5

Cut out the pieces along the tracing lines.

6

Transfer any placement and detail stitching lines to the right side of the fabric using a light box and a pencil.

POSITION AND FUSE APPLIQUÉ PIECES

1

Remove the paper backing from all of the appliqué pieces *except* the cats. Refer to the photo or schematic for placement.

2

Position all spots, stripes, ears, noses, and whites of eyes on their corresponding cat. Fuse. Note that the Summer cat doesn't have eyes and the Winter cat gets fewer spots because of the scarf. Trim the stripes on the cats' tails so they are even with the edges of the tail.

3

Position pupils atop the eyes. Fuse. Fuse the tongue on the Spring cat.

4

When all of the pieces have cooled, remove the paper backing from each of the cats.

5

Position the Spring cat on the fuchsia background. Also position the tulip blossom and stem and the bird and beak. Fuse all into place.

6

Position all of the appliqué pieces for the Summer cat onto the deep yellow background. Position the sun and fuse. Fuse the blue sections of the ball on top of the ball and the sunglasses on top of the cat after fusing the other pieces.

7

Repeat this procedure with the remaining cats, the Autumn cat to the violet background and the Winter cat to the deep green background.

8

Use a permanent black marker to color in the bird's pupils.

ASSEMBLING THE QUILT TOP
Sashing

1

To make the sashing, stitch one lime green strip between two medium blue strips. Press seams toward the medium blue. Repeat with remaining strips, for a total of four strips.

2

Cut these strips into 13½" lengths; you will need a total of 12.

3

Stitch a length to both the tops and bottoms of the Spring and Summer Cat blocks. Press seams toward the sashing.

4

To the bottom sashing on the Spring Cat block, stitch the top of the Autumn Cat block. To the bottom of the Summer cat sashing, stitch the top of the Winter Cat block.

5

To the bottoms of the Autumn and Winter Cat blocks, stitch another sashing piece.

6

To one end of each six remaining sashings, attach a corner square. Connect two of these with a square in the center. Repeat this with the two remaining sashings. You will now have three double sets of sashing.

7

Complete the quilt top by connecting these double sets of sashing to the two rows of appliqué blocks. Press seams toward the sashing.

QUILTING

Sandwich the batting between the quilt top and backing, wrong sides together, and baste through all layers, smoothing the quilt top outward from the center. I used a matching thread to quilt the backgrounds of the appliqué blocks and stitched in all of the "ditches." Use wavy quilting lines vertically for the Spring and Winter Cat blocks and horizontally for the Summer and Autumn cats, breaking the path over all appliqué shapes.

Refer to General Instructions on page 9 for binding the wallhanging.

BUTTONHOLE STITCH APPLIQUÉ

1

Use a machine blanket/buttonhole stitch and black machine embroidery thread to stitch over all of the raw edges of the appliqués.

2

The detail lines of the legs are also stitched this way. You may also do a blanket/buttonhole stitch by hand, using either a size 5 or 8 black perle cotton thread, or two strands of six-strand embroidery floss.

3

Some of the detail lines were stitched with a machine triple stitch. These include the mouth and nose lines of the cats, the bird's legs, and part of the outline of the Autumn cat's hat. A triple stitch is basically a straight stitch that repeats itself, causing an embroidered effect. This can be done simply by using a straight stitch, then backstitch, repeat stitching in the same path; backstitch again, and repeat stitching in the same path.

Wavy quilting lines

Tulip Garden, 1998, 57" x 57"
Designed by Patrick Lose.
Quilt top made by Lenny Houts.
Quilted by Nan Wakefield.

TULIP GARDEN

I designed most of the projects for this book during the months of the year that are colder here in Iowa. Working on this one gave me a bad case of spring fever. Although this version definitely reminds me of tulips in full bloom, you can change the look of the quilt completely by turning the block on point. Imagine the southwestern feel you could achieve by doing this and using the colors of a desert sunset.

REQUIRED FABRIC AND SUPPLIES

6 yards deep green: 2½ yards for quilt top, 3½ yards for backing and binding

⅞ yard fuchsia

⅞ yard yellow

⅞ yard medium green

¾ yard lime green

Binding and backing: deep green fabric listed above

Thin cotton batting: 63" x 63"

Thread for piecing

Matching threads for machine quilting

CUTTING FABRICS

Using a rotary cutter, mat, and ruler, cut the following strips selvage to selvage:

DEEP GREEN
Twelve 1½" x 44" strips

Eleven 2½" x 44" strips. From the 2½" strips, cut two hundred 2½" x 2½" squares.

Eight 3½" x 44" strips. Set the strips aside for the border.

Seven 2⅛" x 44" strips for binding

Cut and piece backing to measure 63" x 63"

FUCHSIA
Two 1½" x 44" strips

Ten 2½" x 44" strips. From the 2½" strips, cut one hundred and fifty-six 2½" x 2½" squares.

YELLOW
Two 1½" x 44" strips

Nine 2½" x 44" strips. From the 2½" strips, cut one hundred and forty-four 2½" x 2½" squares.

MEDIUM GREEN
Eighteen 1½" x 44" strips. From one of the strips, cut twenty-five 1½" x 1½" squares.

From fifteen of the remaining strips, cut sixty 1½" x 9½" strips for the sashing. Set the remaining two strips aside for the Nine Patch border blocks.

LIME GREEN
Fifteen 1½" x 44" strips. From two of these, cut thirty-six 1½" x 1½" squares.

From ten of the remaining strips, cut:

One hundred 1½" x 4½" strips to be used in the Tulip blocks.

The remaining strips will be used to strip piece the Nine Patch border blocks.

ASSEMBLING PIECED BLOCKS

1

Stitch two sets of a 1½" strip of fuchsia to a 1½" strip of deep green. Repeat with two sets of a 1½" strip of yellow to a 1½" strip of deep green. (You will have a total of four strip sets.) Press seams toward the deep green. Using your rotary cutter, mat, and ruler, cut these strips into fifty-two 1½" segments of fuchsia and deep green, and forty-eight 1½" segments of yellow and deep green.

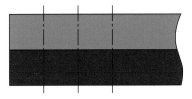

Cut 1½" segments

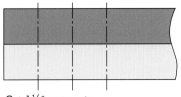

Cut 1½" segments

2

Stitch the remaining 1½" deep green strips together into four sets of green strips. From these, cut one hundred 1½" segments made of two deep green squares as in Step 1.

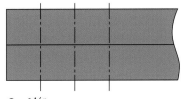

Cut 1½" segments

3

Stitch all of these deep green segments to all of the fuchsia-deep green and yellow-deep green segments. Press.

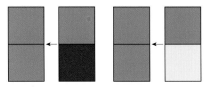

4

From the total number of 2½" squares, set aside fifty-two of the fuchsia squares and forty-eight of the yellow. The remainder—104 squares of fuchsia, 200 squares of deep green, and 96 squares of yellow—is stitched into half-square triangles.

5

To make the half square triangles, lay one fuschia square atop a dark green square with raw edges aligning exactly. Stitch from corner to corner. Using a rotary cutter, mat, and ruler, cut ¼" beyond the diagonal stitching line as shown. Press seams toward the green. Make a total of 104 squares.

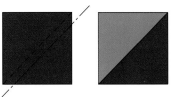

Cutting line

6

Stitch all the yellow squares to the deep green squares in this same manner. Press seams toward the green. Make a total of 96 squares.

7

Stitch corners of the fuchsia Tulip blocks incorporating the fuchsia squares that were set aside in Step 4. Stitch and press seams as shown.

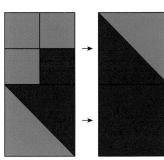

8

Stitch corners of yellow Tulip blocks in this same manner.

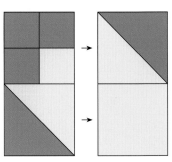

9

Stitch one 1½" × 4½" lime green strip between two of the fuchsia Tulip block corners. Repeat using all fuchsia Tulip block corners. Press seams toward the sashing.

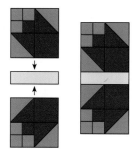

10

Repeat Step 9 using yellow Tulip block corners.

11

Stitch a 1½" medium green square between two 1½" × 4½" lime green strips. Repeat with remaining strips, for a total of 25 strips.

12

Stitch as shown to complete all of the fuchsia and yellow Tulip blocks. Press seams toward the sashing. The blocks should measure 9½" × 9½".

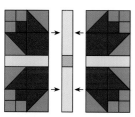

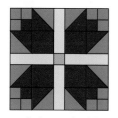

13 fuchsia Tulip blocks

12 yellow Tulip blocks

ASSEMBLING THE QUILT TOP

1

Stitch the 1½" × 9½" medium green strips for the sashing between the five blocks. Begin and end the vertical row with a fuchsia block. Complete three rows in this order. Complete two rows that begin and end with yellow blocks. Press seams toward sashing. Set these aside.

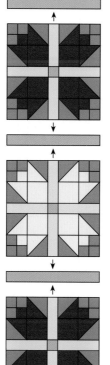

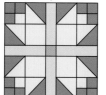

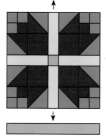

2

To create the vertical sashing, stitch 1½" lime green squares between 1½" × 9½" medium green strips. Begin and end with a lime green square and use five sashing strips to complete six vertical rows of sashing.

3

Stitch all of the Tulip block rows together with a row of vertical sashing between them. Be sure to alternate rows by the color of Tulip block that they begin and end with.

ASSEMBLING THE BORDER
Nine Patch Block

1

Cut the remaining 1½" medium green and lime green strips in half. Stitch three of the strips together in the following order: two medium green strips with a lime green strip between them. Repeat this using two lime green strips with a medium green strip between them. Press all of the seams toward the medium green. Cut these strips, as shown, into 1½" segments.

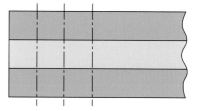

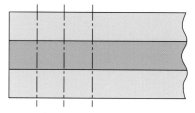

Cut 1½" segments

2

Stitch the segments together to form eight Nine Patch blocks. Assemble them so that four of the blocks have lime green corners and four have medium green corners.

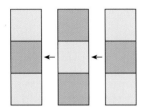

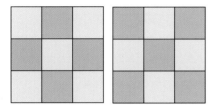

3

Stitch one of the Nine Patch blocks with lime green corners between two deep green border strips. Repeat for a second side border. Press the seams toward the deep green.

5

Stitch the left border to the quilt top, making sure that the Nine Patch block is centered on the lime green strip in the fuchsia Tulip block. Extend the side borders beyond the top and bottom edges of the quilt and, once they are stitched, cut off the overhang flush with these edges. Use a rotary cutter, mat, and ruler in order to make them square. Repeat with the right border. Press seams toward the border.

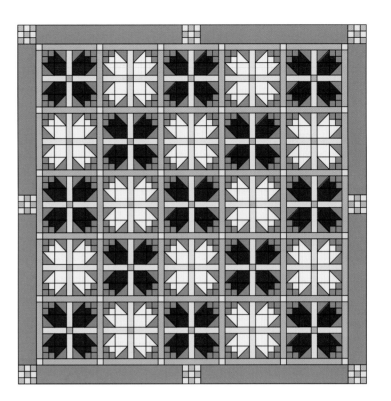

6

Measure the width of the top and bottom of the quilt from one border seam to the other. Add ½" to each measurement. Trim the excess from the remaining two border sections (with the Nine Patch block centered), so that they are the same length as the distance measured between the border seams.

7

To each end of the border sections, stitch a Nine Patch block with medium green corners. Press seams toward the border.

8

Stitch the top border to the quilt top, centering the Nine Patch block in the same manner, matching all other seams. Stitch. Repeat with the bottom border. Press seams toward the border.

9

Sandwich the batting between the quilt top and backing, wrong sides together, and baste through all layers, smoothing the quilt top from the center.

QUILTING

Quilt "in the ditch" along the seams between the sashing and block borders. Quilt the sashing with a wavy line. Stitch cross diagonal lines through the squares and the Nine Patch blocks. With matching thread, quilt ¼" inside the tulips. Quilt the border with a double row of wavy lines. Refer to General Instructions on page 9 for binding instructions.

CALYPSO

Bright, summery colors and shining sun motifs make this cheerful runner a perfect decoration for your next warm weather gathering. It's a quick and easy project that's just right for making on a rainy day when you could use a little sunshine.

Calypso, 1998, 18" x 54"
Designed by Patrick Lose.
Made by Lenny Houts.

REQUIRED FABRICS AND SUPPLIES

Yellow: 1 fat quarter for sun spirals and rays, stars, and stripes

Orange: 1 fat quarter for border diamonds

Lime green: ½ yard for striped blocks, binding, and wavy border appliqué on short sides

Medium blue: ⅜ yard for sun blocks and corner blocks

Fuchsia: 1⅔ yards for borders and backing

Binding: lime green fabric listed above

Backing: fuchsia fabric listed above

Thin cotton batting: 22" x 58"

1 yard lightweight paper-backed fusible adhesive, suitable for sewing

Thread for piecing

Matching machine embroidery threads for satin stitching

Monofilament or matching thread for quilting

CUTTING FABRICS

Using a rotary cutter, mat, and ruler, cut the following pieces:

MEDIUM BLUE
Three 12½" x 12½" background Sun blocks

Four 3½" x 3½" corner squares

LIME GREEN
Two 6½" x 12½" striped background blocks

Four 2⅛" x 44" strips, selvage to selvage, for the binding

FUCHSIA
Two 3½" x 48½", lengthwise, for long borders

Two 3½" x 12½" for short borders

One 22" x 58" piece for backing

FUSIBLE APPLIQUÉ PREPARATION

All appliqué pattern pieces for this project are on pages 59-61. They are printed actual size and reversed for tracing onto fusible adhesive. Refer to page 7 for instructions on fusible appliqué. The wavy stripes and border patterns have been dissected to fit the page. Join the pieces when tracing as indicated on the pattern.

1

Lay the fusible adhesive, paper side up, over each pattern piece and use a pencil to trace onto the paper side. Write the pattern name on each piece as you trace.

2

Use paper cutting scissors to roughly cut all the pieces approximately ¼" outside the traced lines.

3

Then, following manufacturer's instructions for fusing, fuse the traced pattern onto the wrong side of the fabric indicated by color.

YELLOW
3 sun spirals; 44 sun rays; 6 stripes; 4 stars

ORANGE
16 diamonds

LIME GREEN
2 wavy border pieces

4

Cut out the pieces along the tracing lines.

POSITION AND FUSE APPLIQUÉ PIECES

1

Cut out appliqué pieces and remove the paper backing.

2

Lay the yellow stripes on the lime green background blocks, spacing them evenly and alternating their direction. The outer stripes should be approximately ½" from the long raw edges of the blocks. When you are satisfied with their placement, fuse them to the blocks.

3

Center a sun spiral on each of the three larger medium blue blocks, referring to the photo or illustration for placement. Fuse.

4

Arrange 14 of the sun rays evenly around each of the sun spirals. Place each ray about ½" away from the spiral. Fuse.

5

Place the wavy border appliqué piece atop each of the short fuchsia borders, aligning the straight raw edges. Fuse.

6

Center a star on each of the four smaller medium blue corner squares. Each point of the star should be approximately ½" from the raw edges of the square.

7

Set aside the orange diamond appliqué pieces.

ASSEMBLING THE TABLE RUNNER TOP

1

Stitch the lime green side of one of the short borders to one of the Sun blocks. Complete the assembly of the central part of the table runner, as shown. Press all seams toward the Sun blocks.

2

Stitch one corner square to each end of the long fuchsia borders. Press seams toward the corner square.

3

Stitch the long borders to the long sides of the table runner, matching the seams. Press these seams toward the border.

4

After assembling the top, arrange the orange diamonds, end to end lengthwise, down the length of the fuchsia border. Keep the points ¼" away from the raw edge of the border so that they won't be covered by the binding.

5

Fuse diamonds in place.

6

Sandwich the batting between the table runner top and backing, wrong sides together, and baste through all layers.

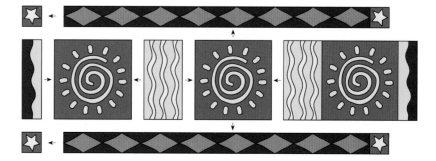

QUILTING

Before you begin satin stitching, quilt seams "in the ditch" with monofilament or matching quilting thread.

SATIN STITCH APPLIQUÉ

1

Using matching thread suitable for machine appliqué, satin stitch around the center block sun spiral. To satin stitch, use a fairly narrow zigzag stitch and keep your stitch length as close as possible. Stitch over the raw edges of the fused appliqué pieces so that none of the raw edges show.

2

Next, satin stitch around all of the rays in the center Sun block. Working outward from the center and smoothing the fabric as you proceed, move to the stripes in the adjacent lime block. Begin stitching the stripe closest to center and move outward.

3

Repeat with the other striped block. Stitch the remaining Sun blocks.

4

Change thread colors and stitch the wavy raw edge of the appliqué in the short borders.

5

Change to orange thread. Refer to the illustration; follow the stitching path in the direction of the arrows to satin stitch the border diamonds. Refer to General Instructions on page 9 to bind the table runner.

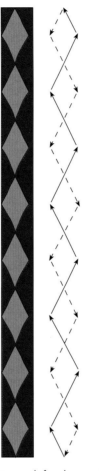

Stitching path for diamonds

Woven Rainbow, 1998, 58" x 58"
Designed by Patrick Lose. Quilt top made by Shon Jones.
Quilted by Shon Jones and Lenny Houts.

WOVEN RAINBOW

I can't think of a better display of color than a rainbow, and this rainbow-themed quilt is easy to piece, using 8" blocks in a basket weave formation. Rotary cutting and basic strip piecing make the quilt top come together quickly, giving you more time to concentrate on the fun part—quilting it!

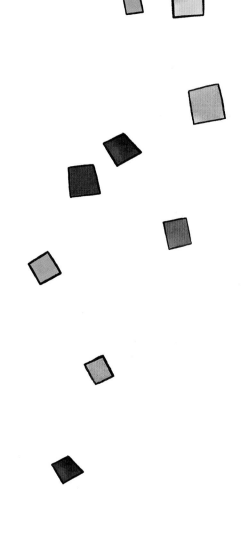

REQUIRED FABRICS AND SUPPLIES

5⅝ yards deep blue: 2 yards for quilt top, 3⅝ yards for backing

1 yards medium blue (includes binding)

¾ yard yellow

½ yard orange-red

½ yard orange

½ yard medium green

Binding: medium blue fabric listed above

Backing: deep blue fabric listed above

Thin cotton batting: 64" x 64"

Thread for piecing

Monofilament or matching thread for quilting

CUTTING FABRICS

Using a rotary cutter, mat, and ruler, cut the following strips selvage to selvage:

DEEP BLUE
Fifteen 2½" x 44" strips

Sixteen 1½" x 44" strips for the border

Cut and piece backing to measure 64" x 64"

MEDIUM BLUE
Eight 1½" x 44" strips for the blocks and border

Six 2⅛" x 44" strips for the binding

YELLOW
Eight 1½" x 44" strips for the blocks and border

One 9½" x 44" strip. From the 9½" strip, cut four 9½" x 9½" corner squares.

ORANGE-RED
Eight 1½" x 44" strips for the blocks and border

ORANGE
Eight 1½" x 44" strips for the blocks and border

MEDIUM GREEN
Eight 1½" x 44" strips for the blocks and border

ASSEMBLING PIECED BLOCKS

1

Three of the fifteen 2½" strips of deep blue are used for each colorway in the blocks. (Five colorways = fifteen strips total of the deep blue.) Between each set of three deep blue strips, stitch two of the 1½" strips of each color (orange-red, orange, yellow, medium green, and medium blue). Press seams toward the deep blue.

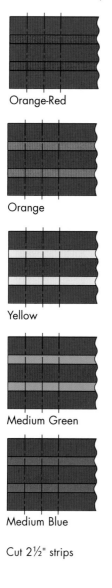

Orange-Red

Orange

Yellow

Medium Green

Medium Blue

Cut 2½" strips

2

Using your rotary cutter, mat, and ruler, cut each of these pieced strips into fifteen 2½" strips as shown. There will be approximately 6½" of remaining fabric that will not be used.

3

Cut two of the eight 1½" strips from each of the five colors (orange-red, orange, yellow, medium green, and medium blue) into 8½" lengths.

4

To sew each block, refer to illustrations. Press seams toward the narrow strips. Make five blocks for each colorway: a total of twenty-five 8½" blocks.

Orange-Red   5 blocks

Orange   5 blocks

Yellow   5 blocks

Medium Green   5 blocks

Medium Blue   5 blocks

5

Referring to the photo or schematic, assemble the blocks, one horizontal row at a time. Note that the seamless 1"-wide (finished) strips of color run either horizontally or vertically, alternating. This alternating pattern creates the "basket weave" effect. Press the seams in one direction. Press seams in opposite direction in alternating rows. As each row is completed, stitch it to the previous row, matching all seams. Press seams in one direction.

ASSEMBLING THE BORDER

1

Sew the remaining 1½" strips of all colors (including deep blue) together in four sets as follows:

Stitch the long edges of a deep blue strip to an orange-red strip. To the other side of the deep blue, stitch an orange strip. To the other side of the orange, stitch another deep blue strip.

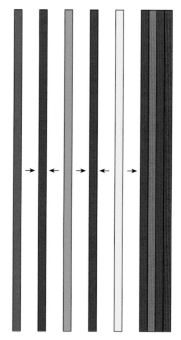

Continue in this manner with yellow next, then medium green, and ending with medium blue. Press seams.

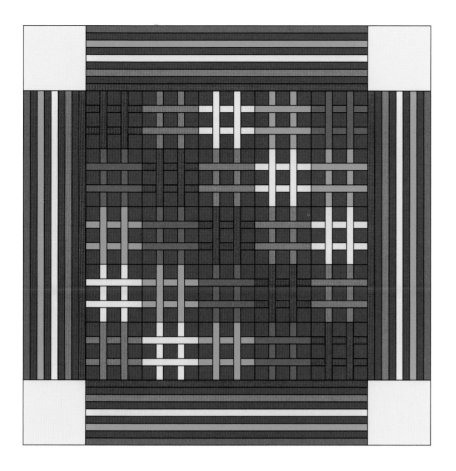

2

To opposite sides of the quilt, stitch a border, positioning the orange-red side of the border to the quilt top. Extend the side borders beyond the top and bottom edges of the quilt and, once they are stitched, cut off the overhang, flush with these edges. Use a rotary cutter, mat, and ruler in order to make them square.

3

Measure the width of the top and bottom of the quilt from one border seam to the other. Add ½" to each measurement. Trim the excess from the remaining two border sections, so that they are the same length as the distance measured between the border seams.

4

To each end of the border sections, stitch one of the 9½" yellow squares. Press seams toward the border.

5

Stitch these borders to the top and bottom of the quilt, matching seams. Press seams toward the border.

6

Sandwich the batting between the quilt top and backing, wrong sides together, and baste through all layers, smoothing the quilt top outward from the center.

QUILTING

Using monofilament thread, I stitched in all the ditches, following the lines of the basket weaving and of the border stripes. As I stitched the border stripes, I did a continuation of the same lines for the four corner blocks. Refer to General Instructions on page 9 for binding instructions.

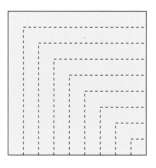

Corner quilting lines

Special Delivery, 1998, 44" x 44"
Designed by Patrick Lose.
Made and quilted by Lenny Houts.

SPECIAL DELIVERY

Upon showing this quilt to dozens of family members, friends, and colleagues familiar with my work, I never failed to get the same responses. First came the standard reaction to anything made for babies…"Awwww, that's soooo cute!" and "Isn't that adorable!?" Then came the reaction of surprise to the idea that I would design anything in pastel colors. It's true; I usually tend to stay on the brighter side of the spectrum. But I love to work in pastel shades as well, especially if they still retain some of the true color from which they paled. Not to mention the fact that I have a special place in my heart for babies. I hope you like this piece from my walk on the "mild" side.

REQUIRED FABRICS AND SUPPLIES

Aqua: 2 yards for pieced border, letters, and backing

Light blue: 1⅓ yards for sky background, 4 stripes and 2 bows on rattles, and binding

Lavender: ½ yard for top and bottom border with words

Mint green: ½ yard for bunting, pieced border, and letters

Medium blue: ¼ yard for corner squares and hat top

Light yellow: 1 fat quarter for stars and rattles

White: ⅝ yard for stork

Butterscotch: 4" x 11" piece for stork's beak

Black: 4" x 11" piece for stork's hat visor, and pupils

Light pink: 7" x 10" piece for stork's hat band, 2 bows, and 4 stripes on rattles

Buff: 8" x 9" piece for baby's face, feet, and hands

Binding: light blue fabric listed at left

Backing: aqua fabric listed at left

Thin cotton batting: 48" x 48"

1¾ yard ✳ lightweight paper-backed fusible adhesive, suitable for sewing

Thread for piecing

Matching machine embroidery threads for satin stitching

Monofilament or matching thread for quilting

CUTTING FABRICS

Using your rotary cutter, mat, and ruler, cut the following pieces:

LIGHT BLUE
One 32½" x 32½" square for sky background

Five 2⅛" x 44" strips, selvage to selvage, for binding

LAVENDER
Two 6½" x 32½" pieces for top and bottom border

MEDIUM BLUE
Four 6½" x 6½" corner squares

MINT GREEN
Three 2½" x 44" strips, selvage to selvage, for pieced border

AQUA
Three 2½" x 44" strips, selvage to selvage, for pieced border

Cut and piece backing to measure 48" x 48"

✳ Fusible adhesive may make the quilt stiff. If the quilt will be used by a baby, you may wish to hand appliqué the quilt. However, if you decide to hand appliqué, remember to add the desired seam allowance to the pattern pieces.

FUSIBLE APPLIQUÉ PREPARATION

All appliqué pattern pieces for this project are on pages 62-75. They are printed actual size and reversed for tracing onto fusible adhesive. I have also included a complete alphabet and numbers so you can customize your quilt. To do this replace the word "Special" with baby's name and applique baby's birthdate in place of the word "Delivery." Refer to page 7 for instructions on fusible appliqué.

Several of the pattern pieces in this project have been dissected to fit the page. Connect these, as you trace, by joining the sections indicated on these patterns. The stork is such a large bird that you will not be able to connect his entire body on the sheet of fusible adhesive; therefore, you will need to trace and connect the stork in two parts, as shown. Later, when it comes time to fuse, you will then have to place both parts of the stork on the wrong side of the entire piece of white fabric, aligning the neck to the body, and fusing the complete stork into place.

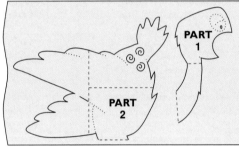

1
Lay the fusible adhesive, paper side up, over each pattern piece and use a pencil to trace onto the paper side. Write the number on each piece as you trace.

2
Be sure to trace any appliqué placement lines or detail stitching lines using a permanent marker.

3
Use paper cutting scissors to roughly cut all the pieces approximately ¼" outside the traced lines.

4
Then, following manufacturer's instructions for fusing, fuse the traced pattern onto the wrong side of the fabric indicated by color.

5
Cut out the pieces along the tracing lines.

6
Transfer any placement and detail stitching lines to the right side of the fabric using a light box and a pencil.

WHITE
1 stork head and neck (S 1); 1 stork body (S 2)

BUTTERSCOTCH
1 stork beak (S 3)

BLACK
1 hat visor (S 4); 1 stork pupil (S 7); 2 baby pupils (S 13)

LIGHT PINK
1 hat band (S 5); 2 lower stripes (S 16); 2 upper stripes (S 17); 2 rattle bows (S 19)

MEDIUM BLUE
1 hat top (S 6)

LIGHT BLUE
2 lower stripes (S 16); 2 upper stripes (S 17); 2 rattle bows (S 19)

MINT GREEN
1 bunting (S 8); 1 bunting tie (S 9); 1 each of the following letters: P, C, A, D, L, V, and R (S 20)

BUFF
1 baby's face (S 10); 1 baby's feet (S 11); 1 baby's arm (S 12)

LIGHT YELLOW
3 large stars (S 14); 3 small stars (S 15); 4 rattles (S 18)

AQUA
1 each of the following letters: S, L, and Y; 3 each of the letter E; 2 each of the letter I (S 20)

ASSEMBLING THE QUILT TOP

Note: With this quilt, you will first need to assemble the entire quilt top, *before* positioning and fusing the appliqué.

Checkerboard Border

1

Start by creating the checkerboard border. Stitch one aqua strip between two mint green strips. Press seams toward the aqua.

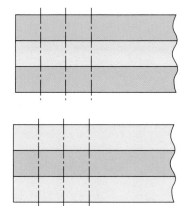

Cut 2½" segments

2

Repeat Step 1 using one mint strip between two aqua strips. Press seams toward the mint.

3

Using your rotary cutter, mat, and ruler, cut the strips into 2½" segments as shown. Keep the two different colored pieced segments separated.

4

Matching seams and raw edges, stitch 16 segments together alternating colors for each side of the quilt. Press seams in one direction.

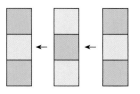

5

To each end of these checkerboard borders, stitch one of the medium blue corner squares. Press seams.

6

To the top and bottom of the light blue background stitch the lavender borders. Press seams toward the borders.

7

Matching seams and raw edges, stitch the checkerboard border with corner squares to the sides of the quilt top. Press seams toward the borders.

POSITION AND FUSE APPLIQUÉ PIECES

1

Referring to the photo or schematic for placement, remove the paper backing and position all appliqué pieces onto the quilt top, overlapping some as necessary.

2

When you are satisfied with positioning, fuse the pieces into place, following the manufacturer's instructions for fusing, making sure that you smooth the larger pieces as you proceed.

SATIN STITCH APPLIQUÉ

1

Sandwich the batting between the quilt top and backing, wrong sides together, and baste through all layers, smoothing the quilt top outward from the center.

2

Beginning at the center of the quilt, using as narrow a stitch width as possible, satin stitch around all of the appliqués using the thread colors you choose. Notice that I used matching thread for all pieces except around the stork, where I used gray, and the features on the baby's face and curly hair, where I used black.

3

Satin stitch the lettering and rattles last. Be sure to stitch any other broken stitching lines such as in the bunting and stork's beak. However, don't satin stitch the broken spiral lines on the stork's back.

QUILTING

I quilted the majority of the quilt with what is commonly called stippling. This is done by using a darning foot and lowering the feed dogs on your machine. Then you stitch free-form squiggly lines that meander through large open areas of the quilt resembling a continuous vermicelli noodle curled on a plate. You can do this as densely as you like in the light blue background and medium blue corner squares around the appliqué motifs.

Stippling quilting lines

Within the stork's body, I quilted the spirals shown on the pattern piece on page 65. The three spirals shown give an idea of the spacing, though I did the spirals "free-hand" and spaced them all over the stork in a similar manner to what is shown. Don't worry about being too precise. Vary the size and spacing to add interest.

The border is quilted with a large grid that is approximately 2¾". This is simple to do if you stitch diagonal lines in both directions through the corners of the aqua squares in the checkerboard. To stitch the grid in the lavender top and bottom borders, simply continue the grid from the sides, using a straight edge to pick up the stitching line on the lavender where you left off in the aqua squares. Then, on the lavender, mark parallel lines that are 2¾" apart. All quilting was done with matching thread. Refer to General Instructions on page 9 for binding instructions.

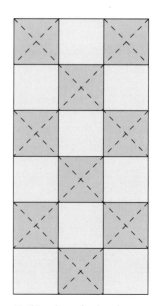

Quilting lines for borders

Twilight Blossoms, 1998, 30" x 8"
Designed by Patrick Lose.
Made by Lenny Houts.

TWILIGHT BLOSSOMS

Once you've experienced how easy it is to make this whimsical door topper, you'll want to make one to place above every door and window in your home. The colors I used are a little more subdued than most of the other projects in this book because I designed this piece to go above a door in my kitchen, which is colored in mostly warm tones. Use your imagination and re-color it to coordinate with the palette in your special rooms.

CUTTING FABRICS

Cut the door topper from the black fabric, following the instructions below. (The remaining black fabric will be used for the backing.) Trace the door topper background pattern from the book onto the tracing paper. The pattern has been dissected into two parts (A and B) to fit the page. Join these sections as you trace, and note that the fold line is the center of the pattern. Fold the black fabric in half, selvage to selvage. Place the tracing paper pattern on the fold; pin and cut.

Cut a 12" x 34" piece from the remaining black fabric for backing. Using a rotary cutter, mat, and ruler, cut two 2⅛" x 44" strips, selvage to selvage, from the light red fabric for the binding.

REQUIRED FABRICS AND SUPPLIES

Black: ⅝ yard for door topper background and backing

Avocado green: ¼ yard for the vine

Burnt orange: 7" x 7" piece for the blossoms

Butterscotch: 6" x 6" piece for the stars

Light red: ⅛ yard for the hearts and binding

Binding: light red fabric listed above

Backing: black fabric listed above

Thin cotton batting: 12" x 34"

¾ yard lightweight paper-backed fusible adhesive, suitable for sewing

Tracing paper at least 10" x 16"

Matching machine embroidery threads for satin stitching

Matching thread for binding

FUSIBLE APPLIQUÉ PREPARATION

All appliqué pattern pieces for this project are on pages 76-81. They are printed actual size and reversed for tracing onto fusible adhesive. Refer to page 7 for instructions on fusible appliqué.

1
Note that the vine pattern (A-D) has been dissected to fit the page. Join the four sections as you trace them onto the paper side of the fusible adhesive.

2
Continue tracing all other pieces, labeling the pattern number on each piece for easy reference later. Be sure to trace the stitching detail lines on the blossoms.

3
Use paper cutting scissors to roughly cut all the pieces approximately ¼" outside the traced lines.

4
Then, following manufacturer's instructions for fusing, fuse the traced pattern onto the wrong side of the fabric indicated by color.

AVOCADO GREEN
1 vine (T 1)

LIGHT RED
1 heart (T 2); 2 hearts (T 3)

BUTTERSCOTCH
**1 star (T 4); 4 stars (T 5);
4 stars (T 6)**

BURNT ORANGE
**2 blossoms (T 7); 2 blossoms (T 8);
2 blossoms (T 9)**

5
Cut out the pieces along the tracing lines.

6
Transfer the detail stitching lines of the blossoms to the right side of the fabric using a light box and a pencil.

POSITION AND FUSE APPLIQUÉ PIECES

1
Don't remove the paper backing from the appliqué pieces until you are ready to place them.

2
Fold the black background in half and lightly finger-crease to establish center. Do the same with the vine appliqué.

3
Remove the backing from the vine and center it on the black background, matching crease lines. Be sure the raw edge of the base of the vine aligns with the raw edge of the base of the background. When you are satisfied with the position, fuse into place.

4
Using the photo or schematic as a guide, position the rest of the appliqué pieces onto the background, noting that the left side of the door topper is a reverse image of the right. It is easier to fuse one piece at a time as you proceed.

SATIN STITCH APPLIQUÉ

1
Sandwich the batting between the door topper and backing, wrong sides together, and baste through all layers.

2
Using matching thread, satin stitch around the vine. To satin stitch, use a fairly narrow zigzag stitch and keep your stitch length as close as possible. Stitch over the raw edges of the fused appliqué pieces so that none of the raw edges show. Working outward from center and smoothing the fabric as you proceed, satin stitch around all of the other appliqué pieces, changing thread colors as necessary.

FINISHING THE DOOR TOPPER

Although I did not quilt my door topper, feel free to do so. Refer to General Instructions on page 9 to bind the door topper. Note that although the edge is curved, it isn't necessary to cut bias binding.

A Perfect Setting, 1998, 18" x 13"
Designed by Patrick Lose.
Made by Lenny Houts.

A PERFECT SETTING

These whimsical placemats will keep your table looking perfectly set all the time. I chose to use bold and bright primary colors that would appeal to children, but you might opt for colors that coordinate with your dining area. If you're feeling especially creative, you might even design a tempting "appliqué entrée" to place on the colorful plate.

REQUIRED FABRICS AND SUPPLIES

Yardage and instructions are given for one placemat.

Deep Blue: ½ yard for the placemat background and backing

White: 8" x 8" piece for plate

Orange-red: ⅓ yard for plate border and binding

Yellow: 6" x 8" piece for plate border triangles and utensil handles

Gray: 5" x 6" piece for utensil tops

Backing: deep blue fabric listed above

Thin cotton batting: 17" x 22"

⅓ yard lightweight paper-backed fusible adhesive, suitable for sewing

Matching machine embroidery threads for satin stitching

Matching thread for binding

Monofilament or matching thread for quilting

CUTTING FABRICS

Using a rotary cutter, mat, and ruler, cut the 13½" x 18½" placemat top from the deep blue fabric. Cut the backing, also from deep blue, 17" x 22".

From the orange-red fabric, cut a 12" x 12" square from one selvage edge. From the length of the remaining fabric, cut two 2⅛"-wide strips the width of the fabric. This will be used for the binding; see Cutting Layout.

Cutting Layout

FUSIBLE APPLIQUÉ PREPARATION

All appliqué pattern pieces for this project are on pages 82-84. They are printed actual size and reversed for tracing onto fusible adhesive. Refer to page 7 for instructions on fusible appliqué.

1
Only one half of the plate border pattern has been printed. Lay the fusible adhesive, paper side up, and trace this pattern, including the folding line, then turn the fusible adhesive to trace the second half (the pattern is symmetrical).

2
Continue tracing all other pattern pieces. Be sure to trace the appliqué placement and detail stitching lines.

3
Use paper cutting scissors to roughly cut all the pieces approximately ¼" outside the traced lines.

4
Then, following manufacturer's instructions for fusing, fuse the traced pattern onto the wrong side of the fabric indicated by color.

WHITE
1 plate

ORANGE-RED
1 plate border

YELLOW
12 plate border triangles; 1 of each fork, knife, and spoon handle

GRAY
1 of each fork, knife, and spoon

5
Cut out all appliqué shapes. When cutting out the plate (white), cut slightly outside of the lines (⅛" or less) in order for the plate border to overlap. This will eliminate the possibility of gaps between the pieces.

6
Transfer the appliqué placement and detail stitching lines to the fabric side using a light box and a pencil. These lines will be covered by satin stitching.

POSITION AND FUSE APPLIQUÉ PIECES

1
Don't remove the paper backing from the appliqué pieces until you have located their position and are ready to place them.

2
Fold the placemat top in half, horizontally, and finger-crease to establish center. Do the same vertically.

QUILTING

To quilt the grid pattern, use a ruler and a Chaco-liner to mark the 1" grid pattern on the background only. Your first line should be drawn at vertical center. From that line, mark lines 1" apart to the right and left. Do the same horizontally. Quilt these lines using matching or monofilament thread. Refer to General Instructions on page 9 to bind the placemats.

3
Remove the backing from the plate (white) and fold it in quarters, lightly finger-creasing. Center the crease lines on the plate over the crease lines on the placemat top and position the plate. Fuse in place.

4
Position the rest of the appliqué pieces onto the background. It's easier to fuse one piece at a time as you proceed.

SATIN STITCH APPLIQUÉ

1
Sandwich the batting between the placemat top and backing, wrong sides together, and baste through all layers.

2
Using deep blue thread, satin stitch the raw edge between the plate and the plate border. To satin stitch, use a fairly narrow zigzag stitch and keep your stitch length as close as possible. Stitch over the raw edges of the fused appliqué pieces so that none of the raw edges show. Working outward from center and smoothing the fabric as you proceed, satin stitch around all of the other appliqué pieces, changing thread colors as necessary.

3
Be sure to stitch the detail lines in the utensils.

PUMPKIN PARTY

These guys are definitely the life of the Halloween party. They were inspired by the antique papier-maché jack-o'-lanterns of the 1920s and 1930s, which seem somber in comparison. I gave them some snazzy threads and expressions that are somewhere between spooky and silly—just right for Halloween.

REQUIRED FABRICS AND SUPPLIES

Orange: 8" x 13" piece for pumpkin faces and candy corn center

Deep yellow: 6" x 8" piece for pumpkin eyes, noses, three of the center pumpkin's teeth, and candy corn bottoms

White: 7" x 10" piece for pumpkin mouths and candy corn tips

Black: ⅛ yard for corner squares, sashing, and rings around the bottom pumpkin's eyes

Assorted prints:
    2" x 3" piece for top pumpkin's hat band

    8" x 10" piece on top and bottom pumpkins' collars

    4" x 9" piece for center pumpkin's collar

Olive green: 2" x 2" piece for pumpkin stems

Violet: 1¼ yard for pumpkin blocks, backing, and binding

Deep orange: ⅓ yard for borders

Binding and backing: violet fabric listed above

Thin cotton batting: 22" x 40"

½ yard lightweight paper-backed fusible adhesive

Thread for piecing

Black machine embroidery thread for satin stitching

Monofilament or matching thread for quilting

Pumpkin Party, 1998, 18" x 36"
Designed by Patrick Lose.
Made and quilted by Lenny Houts.

CUTTING FABRICS

Using a rotary cutter, mat, and ruler, cut the following pieces:

VIOLET
Two Pumpkin blocks 10½" x 8½"

One Pumpkin block 10½" x 12½"

One piece for backing 22" x 40"

Three 2⅛" x 44" binding strips, selvage to selvage

BLACK
Four 3½" x 3½" corner squares

Three 1" x 44" sashing strips, selvage to selvage. From the 1" strip, cut two 30½" lengths and four 10½" lengths.

DEEP ORANGE
Two long borders 3½" x 30½"

Two short borders 3½" x 11½"

FUSIBLE APPLIQUÉ PREPARATION

All appliqué pattern pieces for this project are on pages 85-89. They are printed actual size and reversed for tracing onto fusible adhesive. Refer to page 7 for instructions on fusible appliqué.

1
Lay the fusible adhesive, paper side up, over each pattern piece and use a pencil to trace onto the paper side. Write the pattern number on each piece as you trace.

2
Be sure to trace any appliqué placement lines or detail stitching lines using a permanent marker.

3
Use paper cutting scissors to roughly cut all the pieces approximately ¼" outside the traced lines.

4
Then, following manufacturer's instructions for fusing, fuse the traced pattern onto the wrong side of the fabric indicated by color.

ORANGE
3 pumpkins (P 1-3); 4 candy corn centers (P 4)

DEEP YELLOW
1 of each eye, nose, 3 teeth for center pumpkin, and hat (P 5-17); 4 candy corn bottoms (P 18)

WHITE
1 of each mouth (P 19-21); 4 candy corn tips (P 22)

ASSORTED PRINTS
1 hat band (P 23)
1 of each collar (P 24-25-26)

OLIVE GREEN
1 of each pumpkin stem (P 27-28)

BLACK
1 of each ring around the bottom pumpkin's eyes (P 29-30)

5
Cut out the pieces along the tracing lines.

6
Transfer any placement and detail stitching lines to the right side of the fabric using a light box and a pencil.

POSITION AND FUSE APPLIQUÉ PIECES

1
Don't remove the paper backing from the appliqué pieces until you have located their position and are ready to place them.

2
Note that the long sides of the top and bottom violet Pumpkin blocks are horizontal and the short sides of the center block are horizontal. Remove the backing from the top pumpkin face and center it on the top violet block. Fuse into place.

3
Position the rest of the appliqué pieces onto the background. Overlapping them very slightly (⅟₁₆") will ensure that you don't have any gaps between pieces. When you are satisfied with their positions, fuse all pieces into place.

4
Repeat this procedure with the appliqués for the center and bottom Pumpkin blocks.

5
Fuse the candy corn appliqués to the 3½" black corner squares.

6
Using a permanent black marking pen, color the pupils of the eyes on all eye appliqué pieces.

ASSEMBLING THE BANNER

1
Stitch one of the 10½" sashing strips to the upper edge of the top Pumpkin block.

2
Stitch another 10½" sashing strip to the bottom of the block. Continue this process, until you have all four horizontal sashings pieced. Press all seams toward the sashings.

3
Stitch the remaining lengths to the sides of the banner. Press seams toward the sashing.

4
Stitch the two long orange borders to the sides of the banner. Press seams toward the sashing.

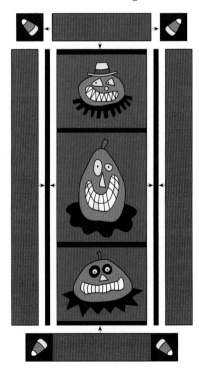

5

Stitch the black corner squares with the candy corn appliqués to the ends of the short orange borders. Note in the photo or schematic, the direction that the candy corn pieces point. Press seams toward the black corner squares.

6

Stitch the short orange top and bottom borders to the banner, matching seams. Press seams toward the sashing.

7

Sandwich the batting between the banner top and backing, wrong sides together, and baste through all layers, smoothing the quilt top outward from the center.

SATIN STITCH APPLIQUÉ

1

All the satin stitching on this banner is done in black embroidery thread. To satin stitch, use a fairly narrow zigzag stitch and keep your stitch length as close as possible. Stitch over the raw edges of the fused appliqué pieces so that none of the raw edges show. Begin with the teeth that you transferred to the mouth of the center pumpkin. Starting with one of the center lines, work outward to each side of the mouth. By beginning with these lines, you will be able to cover the beginnings and endings of the stitching when you outline the mouth.

2

Continue stitching all appliqué shapes in the center pumpkin, working from the center outward and smoothing the fabric as you proceed.

3

Stitch all appliqué shapes in the top and bottom pumpkins, beginning with the teeth as before.

4

Stitch all candy corn appliqués.

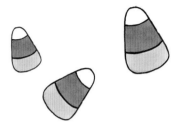

QUILTING

Change to matching thread or monofilament and quilt all seams "in the ditch." Change to matching (violet) or monofilament for quilting the Pumpkin blocks. The Pumpkin blocks are quilted with a wavy grid pattern as shown. The wavy lines are spaced an average of an inch apart (more or less as they curve toward or away from each other).

Quilt the borders of the banner with a meandering path, often referred to as stippling. This is done by using a darning foot and lowering the feed dogs on your machine. Then quilt free-form squiggly lines that meander through large open areas of the quilt.

Refer to General Instructions on page 9 to bind the banner.

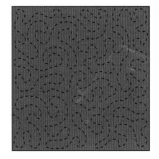

Wavy quilting lines   Stipple quilting lines

Bundled Up, 1998, 35" x 27"
Designed by Patrick Lose.
Made and quilted by Lenny Houts.

BUNDLED UP

What a pair! It looks like this little guy spent a cold day creating a pudgy snowbuddy in his own image. This easy-to-make wall quilt is a perfect holiday decoration that doesn't have to come down with the Christmas tree. The bright, cheery colors will lift your spirits throughout all of those cold, gray days of winter.

REQUIRED FABRICS AND SUPPLIES

White (an opaque white is recommended so dark background does not show through): ¾ yard for snowman, snow, and checkerboard squares for border

Deep blue: 2 yards for background, backing, and checkerboard squares for border

Red: ⅝ yard for boy's coat, boy's earmuffs, inner border, and binding

Green: 5" x 11" piece for corner squares, boy's hat, and boy's mittens

Violet: 5" x 11" piece for snowman's scarf

Golden yellow: 5"x 11" piece for snowman's earmuffs and boy's scarf

Butterscotch: 4" x 7" piece for broom bristles

Light gray: 5" x 7" piece for shovel scoop

Medium blue: 5" x 5" piece for snowman's hat

Buff: 2" x 5" piece for boy's face

Blue-gray: 4" x 7" piece for boy's pants

Black: 8" x 8" piece for boy's boots and coat buttons, snowman's coal buttons, and eyes on both

Gray: 3" x 3" piece for boy's boot buckles

Brown: 4" x 8" piece for broom and shovel handles

Binding: red fabric listed above

Backing: deep blue fabric listed above

Thin cotton batting: 31" x 39"

1¾ yard lightweight paper-backed fusible adhesive

Thread for piecing

Black machine embroidery thread for satin stitching

Matching thread for quilting

CUTTING FABRICS

Using a rotary cutter, mat, and ruler, cut the following pieces:

D E E P   B L U E
One 22½" x 30½" piece for background

Five 1½" x 44" strips, selvage to selvage, for pieced border

One 31" x 39" piece for backing

G R E E N
Four 2½" x 2½" corner squares

W H I T E
Five 1½" x 44" strips, selvage to selvage, for pieced border

R E D
Four 1" x 44" strips, selvage to selvage, for inner border. From the 1" strips, cut two 31½" lengths and two 22½" lengths.

Four 2⅛" x 44" strips, selvage to selvage, for binding

FUSIBLE APPLIQUÉ PREPARATION

All appliqué pattern pieces for this project are on pages 90-101. They are printed actual size and reversed for tracing onto fusible adhesive. Refer to page 7 for instructions on fusible appliqué. Several of the pattern pieces in this project have been dissected to fit the page. Connect these, as you trace, by joining the sections indicated on these patterns.

1
Lay the fusible adhesive, paper side up, over each pattern piece and use a pencil to trace onto the paper side. Write the pattern number on each piece as you trace.

2
Be sure to trace any appliqué placement lines or detail stitching lines using a permanent marker.

3
Use paper cutting scissors to roughly cut all the pieces approximately ¼" outside the traced lines.

4
Then, following manufacturer's instructions for fusing, fuse the traced pattern onto the wrong side of the fabric indicated by color.

W H I T E
1 ground snow (B 1); 1 snowman's body (B 2); 1 large snow mound (B 3); 1 small snow mound (B 4); 1 snowman's face (B 5)

B L A C K
1 pair boots (B 6); 4 jacket buttons (B 7); 2 boy's eyes (B 8); 2 snowman's eyes (B 9); 4 coal buttons (B 10)

RED
1 coat (B 11); 1 arm (B 12); 1 of each
boy's earmuffs (B 13-14)

GOLDEN YELLOW
1 of each snowman's earmuffs
(B 15-16); 1 boy's scarf (B 24)

GREEN
1 hat (B 17); 1 right mitten (B 19);
1 left mitten (B 20)

MEDIUM BLUE
1 hat (B 17)

BUFF
1 boy's face (B 18)

DEEP BLUE-GRAY
1 pair pants (B 21)

BROWN
1 of each shovel handle (B 28-29);
1 of each broom handle (B 30-31)

GRAY
2 left boot buckles (B 22);
2 right boot buckles (B 23)

VIOLET
1 snowman's scarf (B 25)

LIGHT GRAY
1 shovel scoop (B 26)

BUTTERSCOTCH
1 broom bristles (B 27)

5
Cut out the pieces along the tracing
lines.

6
Transfer any placement and detail
stitching lines to the right side of the
fabric using a light box and a pencil.

POSITION AND FUSE APPLIQUÉ PIECES

1
Remove the paper backing from all
of the appliqué pieces. Refer to the
photo or schematic for positioning of
the pieces.

2
Lay the ground snow onto the background, aligning horizontal raw edges.
Fuse. Trim sides of snow even with
the background.

3
Position boots onto ground snow,
referring to placement lines. Fuse.

4
Continue positioning and fusing the
appliqué pieces in the above manner,
noting which pieces overlap others.

ASSEMBLING THE QUILT TOP

1
To each side of the center of the
quilt top, stitch one of the red strips
for the inner border. Press the seams
toward the red.

2
To the top and bottom of the quilt
top, stitch the remaining red strips for
the inner border as in Step 1.

Checkerboard Border

1
Stitch the long side of one deep blue
strip and one white strip together.
Press the seam toward the deep
blue. Repeat for remaining strips.
Using your rotary cutter, mat, and
ruler, cut these strips into 1½" segments as shown.

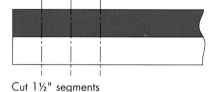

Cut 1½" segments

2
Matching seams and raw edges, stitch
these segments together to form the
checkerboard border. For the top
and bottom borders, stitch thirty-one
segments together. For the side borders, stitch twenty-three segments
together. Press all of the seams to
one side.

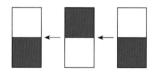

3
To each end of the top and bottom
borders, stitch a green corner square,
pressing the seams toward the green.

4

To each side of the center of the quilt top, stitch one of the checkerboard side borders. Refer to the photo or schematic for color placement. Again, press the seams toward the red inner border. This will "raise" the inner border slightly from the quilt when the quilting is finished.

5

Stitch the long checkerboard borders with the green corner squares to the quilt top. Press the seams toward the red inner border.

6

Sandwich the batting between the quilt top and backing, wrong sides together, and baste through all layers, smoothing the quilt top outward from the center.

SATIN STITCH APPLIQUÉ

1

All satin stitching on this quilt is done in black. I prefer using black thread to make the appliquéd piece look more like a cartoon. Begin satin stitching the detail stitching lines that are within areas of the appliqué pieces. By doing this, you can "hide" the beginnings and ends of your stitching lines when you stitch over the raw edges. For example, start with the lines of the "ribbing" on the cuff of the boy's coat. When those lines are finished, outline the cuff as indicated, stitching over the beginnings and ends of the ribbing lines. Working outward from center and smoothing the fabric as you proceed, satin stitch all detail stitching lines indicated on the appliqué pieces and over all raw edges of the appliqué pieces.

2

The boy's eyes are too small to satin stitch around. To keep them in place permanently, use a straight stitch with black thread and stitch a line from the top to the bottom of the eye. Backstitch at the beginning and the end.

QUILTING

To complete the quilting, I used a matching thread to quilt the sky background. This was done using a darning foot, with the machine's feed dogs lowered, in a meandering "free motion" manner that is often referred to as stippling.

Using matching monofilament thread, stitch "in the ditch" on both sides of the inner border. Also stitch Xs in all of the deep blue squares in the border. Stipple the green corner squares.

Refer to General Instructions on page 9 to bind the wall quilt.

LOVE AND LOYALTY
PROJECT ON PAGE 10

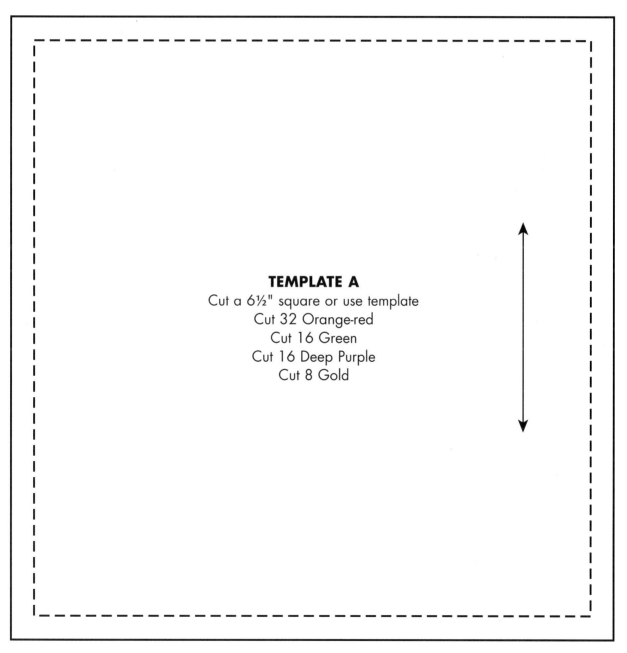

TEMPLATE A
Cut a 6½" square or use template
Cut 32 Orange-red
Cut 16 Green
Cut 16 Deep Purple
Cut 8 Gold

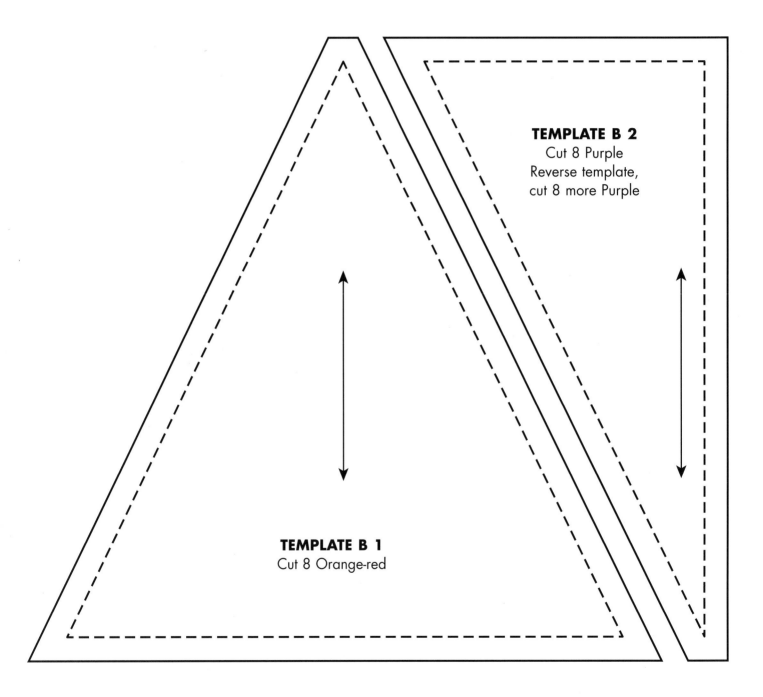

TEMPLATE B 2
Cut 8 Purple
Reverse template,
cut 8 more Purple

TEMPLATE B 1
Cut 8 Orange-red

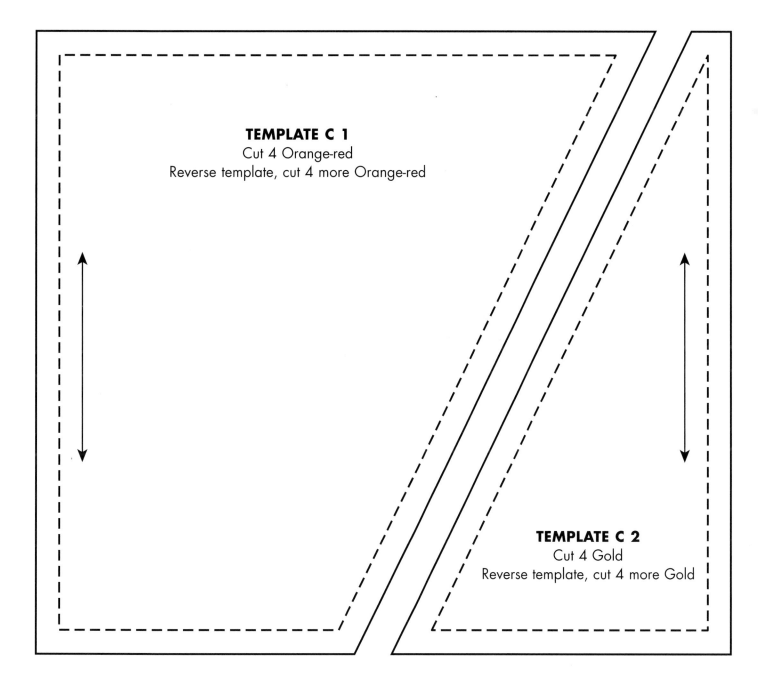

TEMPLATE C 1
Cut 4 Orange-red
Reverse template, cut 4 more Orange-red

TEMPLATE C 2
Cut 4 Gold
Reverse template, cut 4 more Gold

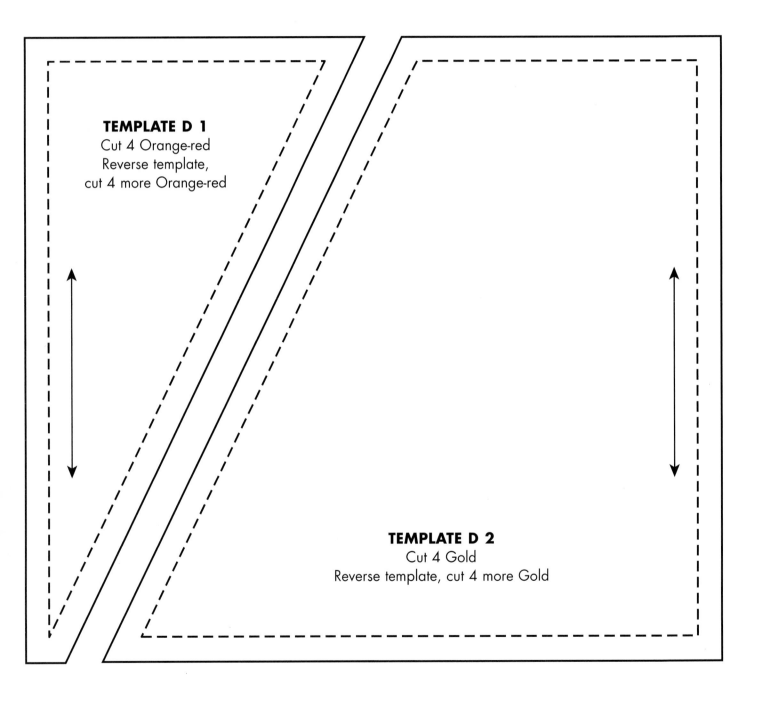

TEMPLATE D 1
Cut 4 Orange-red
Reverse template,
cut 4 more Orange-red

TEMPLATE D 2
Cut 4 Gold
Reverse template, cut 4 more Gold

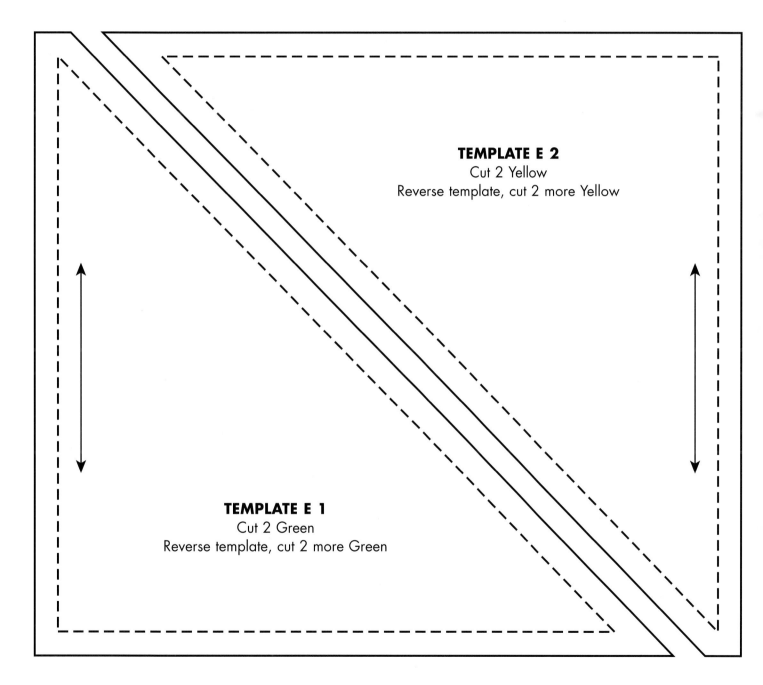

TEMPLATE E 2
Cut 2 Yellow
Reverse template, cut 2 more Yellow

TEMPLATE E 1
Cut 2 Green
Reverse template, cut 2 more Green

A CAT FOR ALL SEASONS

PROJECT ON PAGE 14

← Remove ear
for Autumn cat

**CAT
C 1**
Trace 4

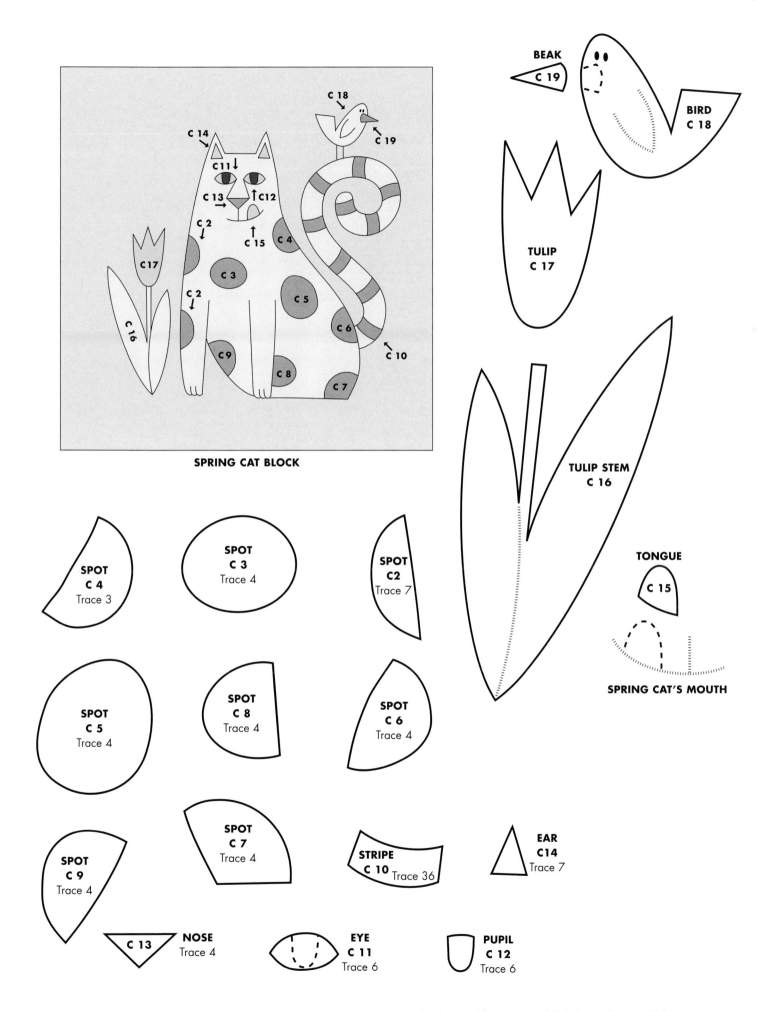

BEAK
C 19

BIRD
C 18

SPRING CAT BLOCK

TULIP
C 17

TULIP STEM
C 16

TONGUE
C 15

SPRING CAT'S MOUTH

SPOT
C 4
Trace 3

SPOT
C 3
Trace 4

SPOT
C2
Trace 7

SPOT
C 5
Trace 4

SPOT
C 8
Trace 4

SPOT
C 6
Trace 4

SPOT
C 9
Trace 4

SPOT
C 7
Trace 4

STRIPE
C 10 Trace 36

EAR
C14
Trace 7

C 13 **NOSE**
Trace 4

EYE
C 11
Trace 6

PUPIL
C 12
Trace 6

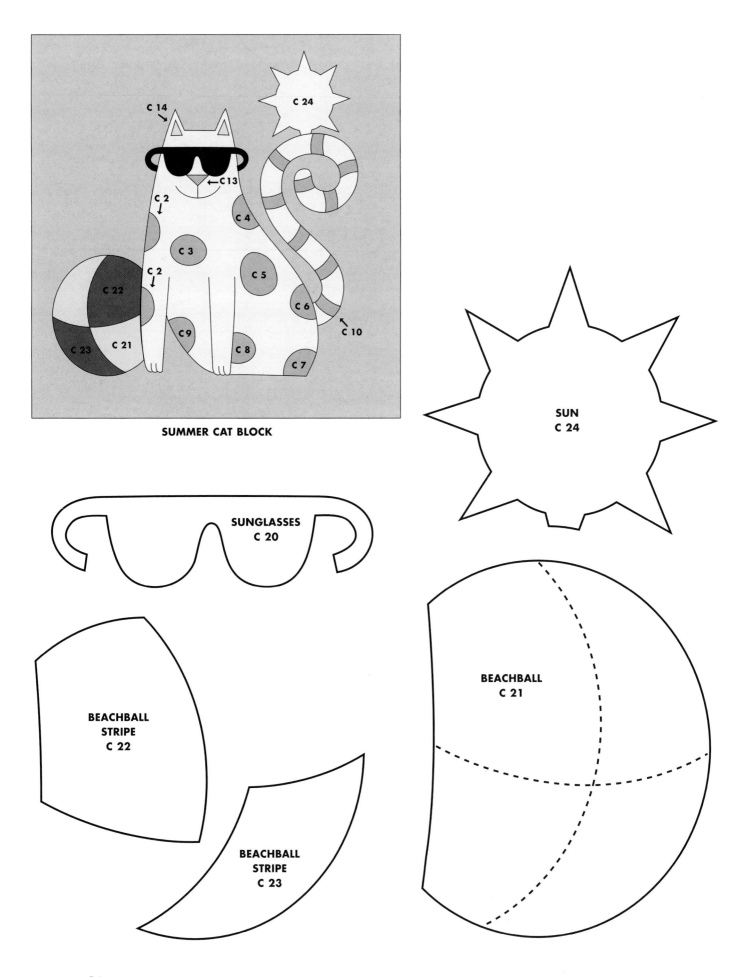

SUMMER CAT BLOCK

SUN C 24

SUNGLASSES C 20

BEACHBALL STRIPE C 22

BEACHBALL STRIPE C 23

BEACHBALL C 21

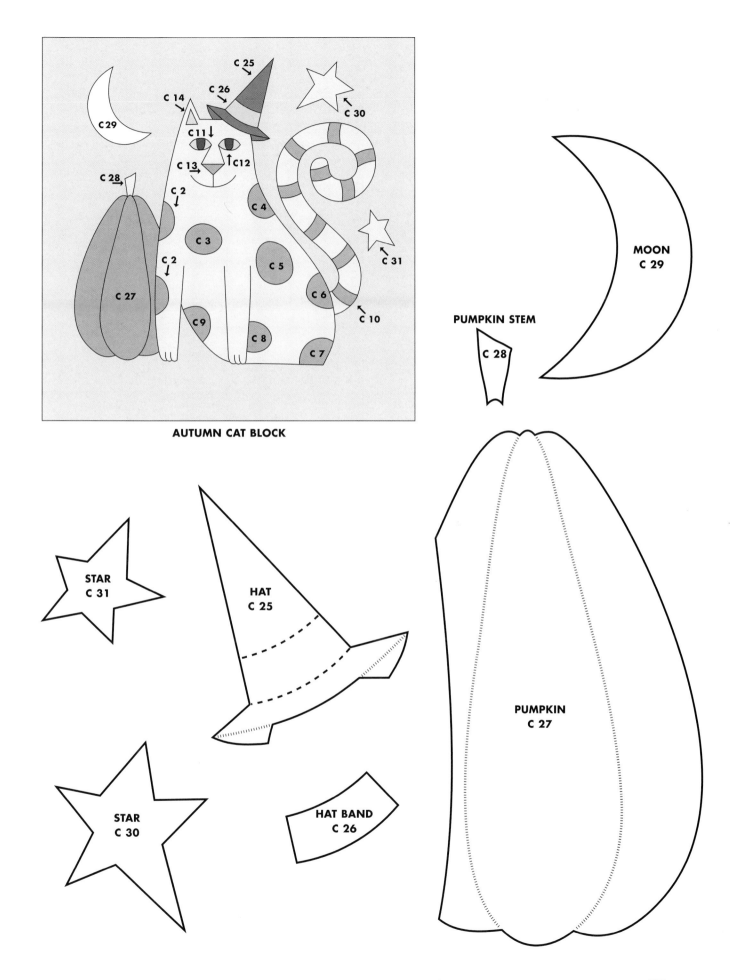

AUTUMN CAT BLOCK

MOON
C 29

PUMPKIN STEM

C 28

STAR
C 31

HAT
C 25

STAR
C 30

HAT BAND
C 26

PUMPKIN
C 27

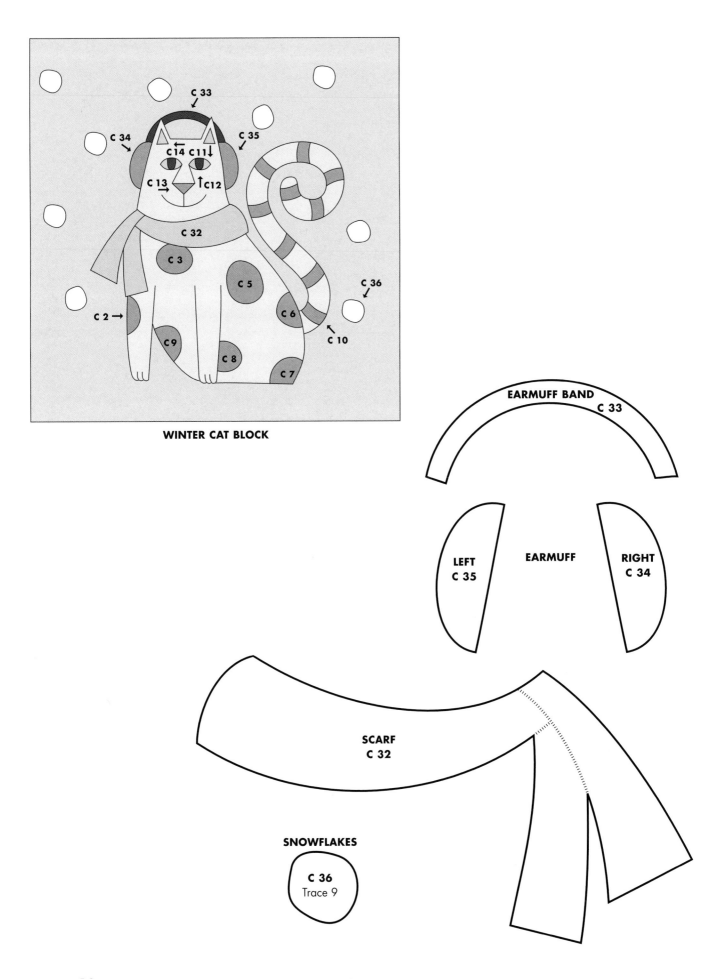

WINTER CAT BLOCK

EARMUFF BAND
C 33

LEFT
C 35

EARMUFF

RIGHT
C 34

SCARF
C 32

SNOWFLAKES

C 36
Trace 9

CALYPSO
PROJECT ON PAGE 24

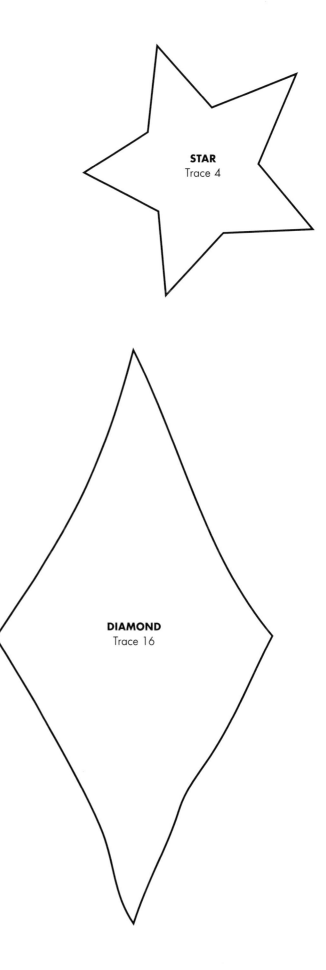

STAR
Trace 4

DIAMOND
Trace 16

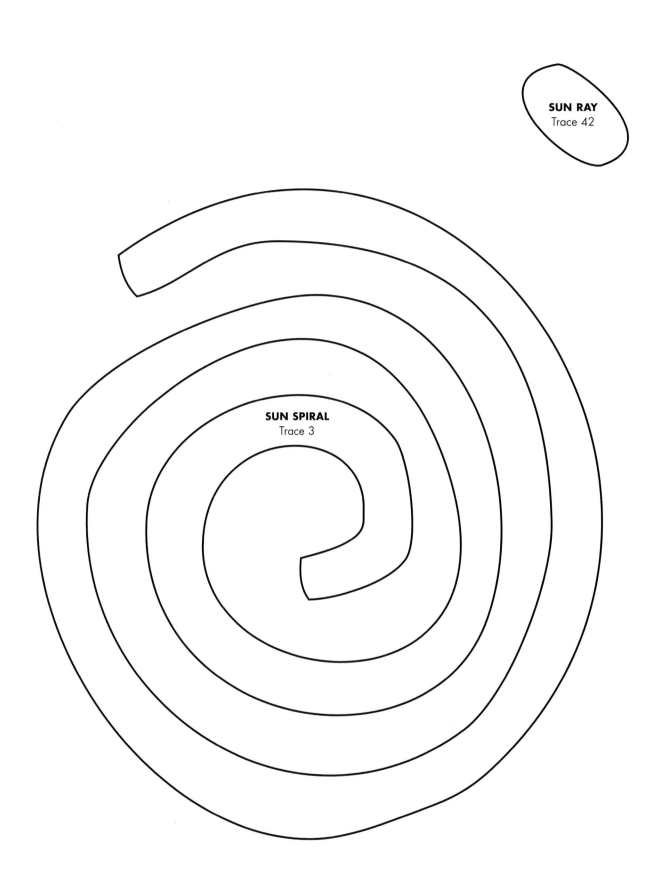

SUN RAY
Trace 42

SUN SPIRAL
Trace 3

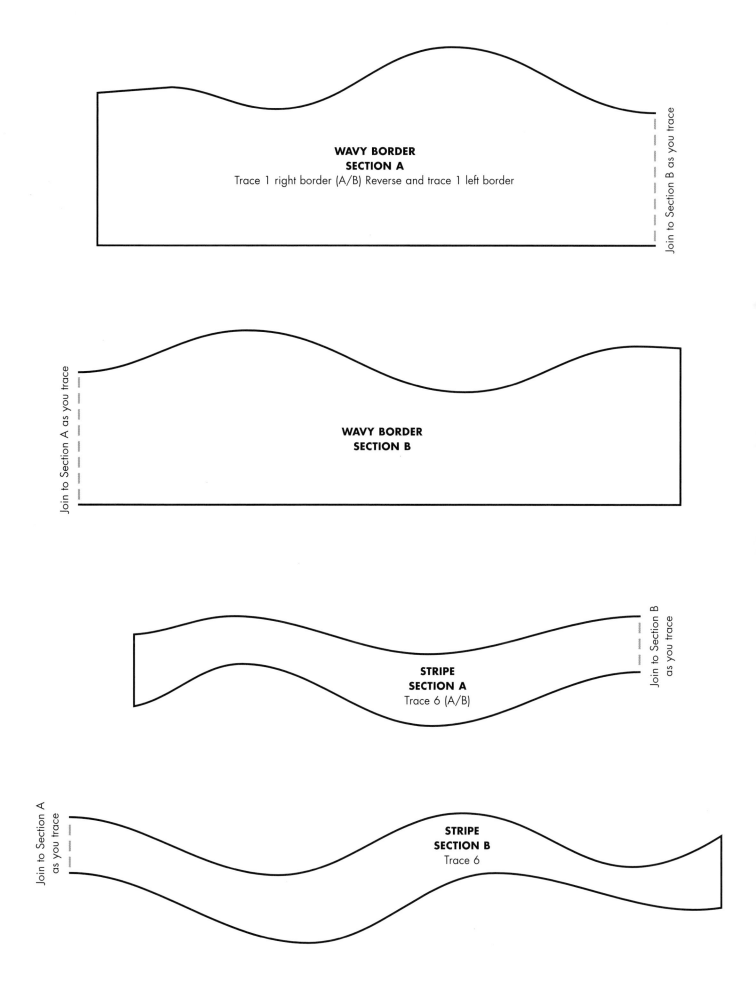

WAVY BORDER
SECTION A
Trace 1 right border (A/B) Reverse and trace 1 left border

Join to Section B as you trace

Join to Section A as you trace

WAVY BORDER
SECTION B

STRIPE
SECTION A
Trace 6 (A/B)

Join to Section B as you trace

Join to Section A as you trace

STRIPE
SECTION B
Trace 6

SPECIAL DELIVERY

PROJECT ON PAGE 32

Special

S 4

S 6

S 9

S 14

S 3

S 7

S 1

S 5

S 13

S 10

S 11

S 12

S 2

S 8

S 15

Delivery

S 17

S 16

S 19

S 18

LETTERS S 20

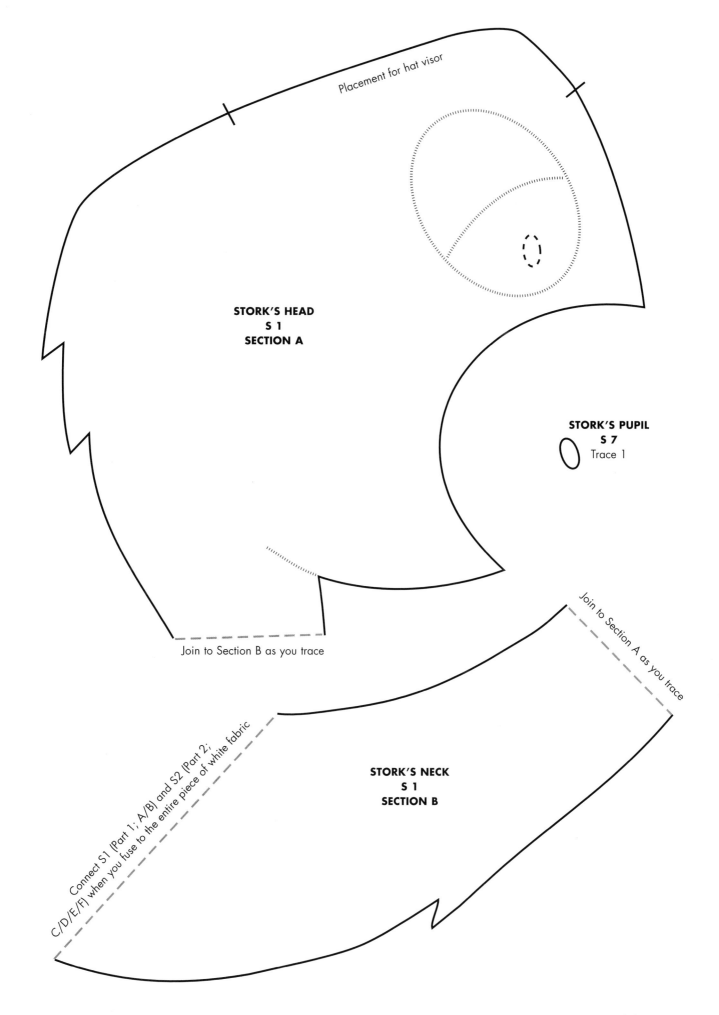

Placement for hat visor

**STORK'S HEAD
S 1
SECTION A**

**STORK'S PUPIL
S 7**
Trace 1

Join to Section B as you trace

Join to Section A as you trace

Connect S1 (Part 1; A/B) and S2 (Part 2; C/D/E/F) when you fuse to the entire piece of white fabric

**STORK'S NECK
S 1
SECTION B**

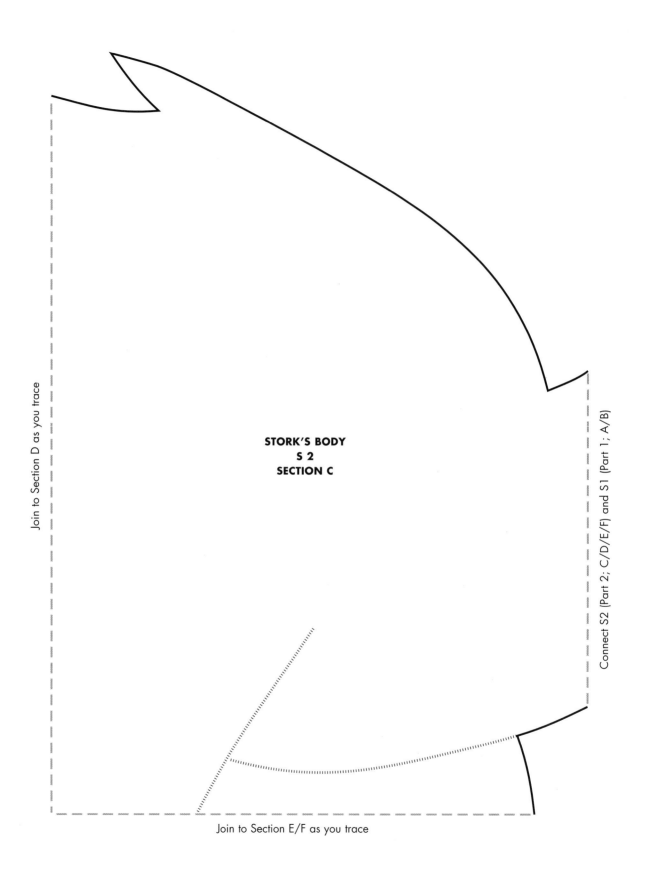

STORK'S BODY
S 2
SECTION C

Join to Section D as you trace

Connect S2 (Part 2; C/D/E/F) and S1 (Part 1; A/B)

Join to Section E/F as you trace

**LARGE STAR
S 14**
Trace 3

**SMALL STAR
S 15**
Trace 3

**STORK'S BODY
S 2
SECTION D**

Join to Section C as you trace

Join to Section E/F as you trace

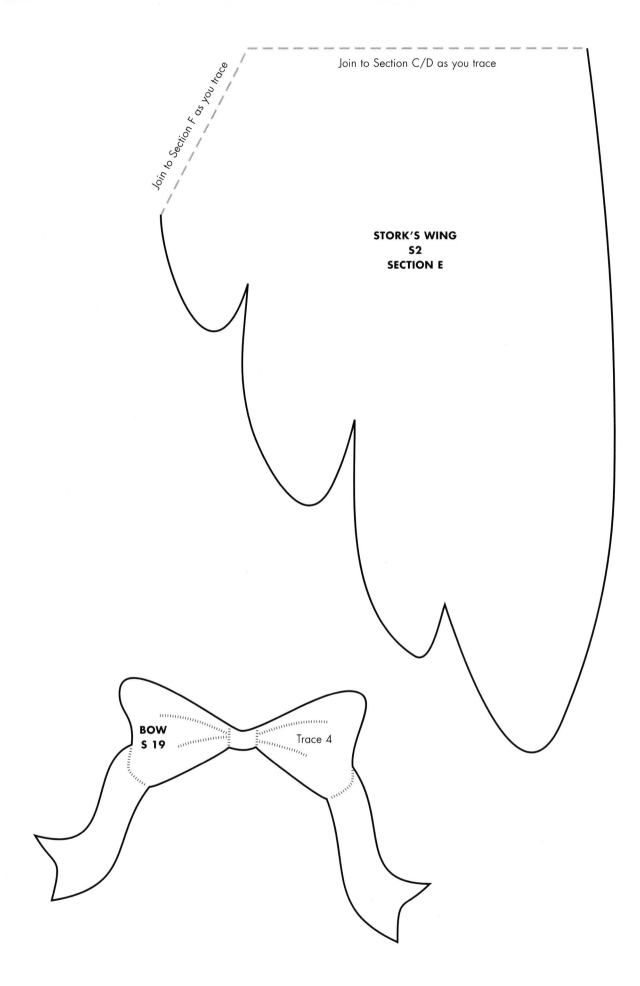

Join to Section F as you trace

Join to Section C/D as you trace

**STORK'S WING
S2
SECTION E**

**BOW
S 19**

Trace 4

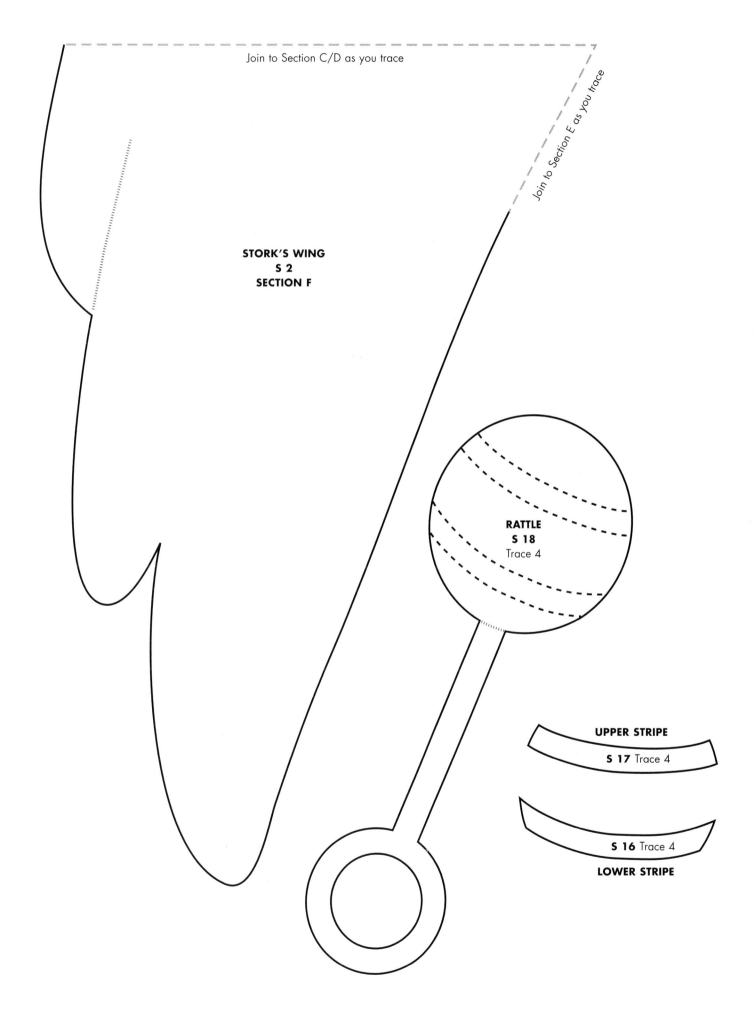

Join to Section C/D as you trace

Join to Section E as you trace

STORK'S WING
S 2
SECTION F

RATTLE
S 18
Trace 4

UPPER STRIPE

S 17 Trace 4

S 16 Trace 4

LOWER STRIPE

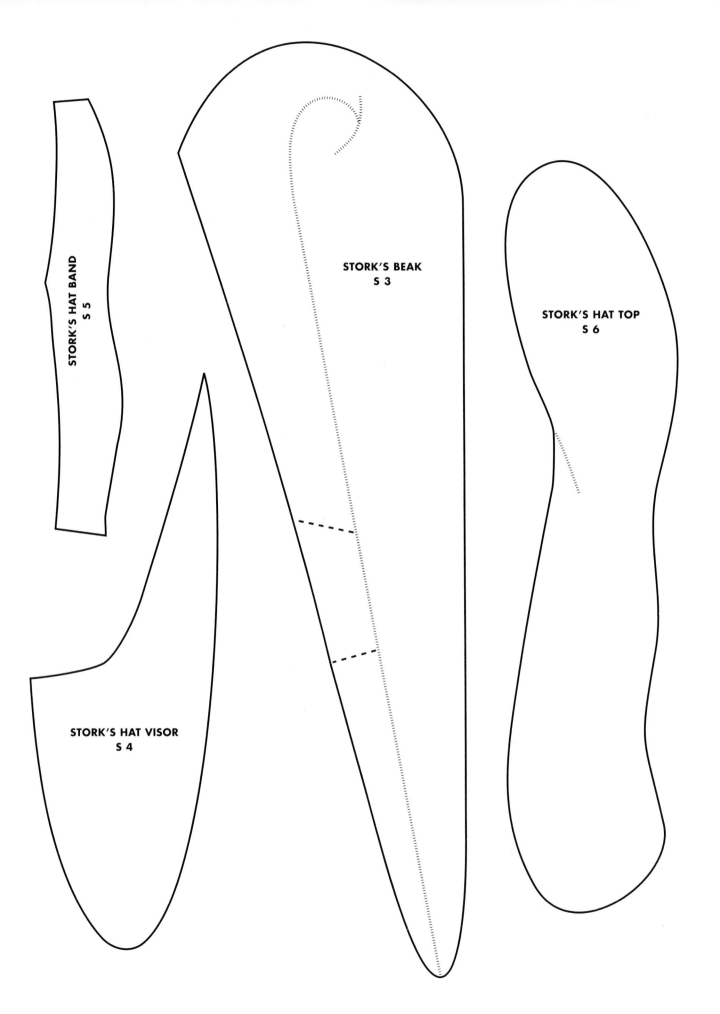

STORK'S HAT BAND
S 5

STORK'S BEAK
S 3

STORK'S HAT TOP
S 6

STORK'S HAT VISOR
S 4

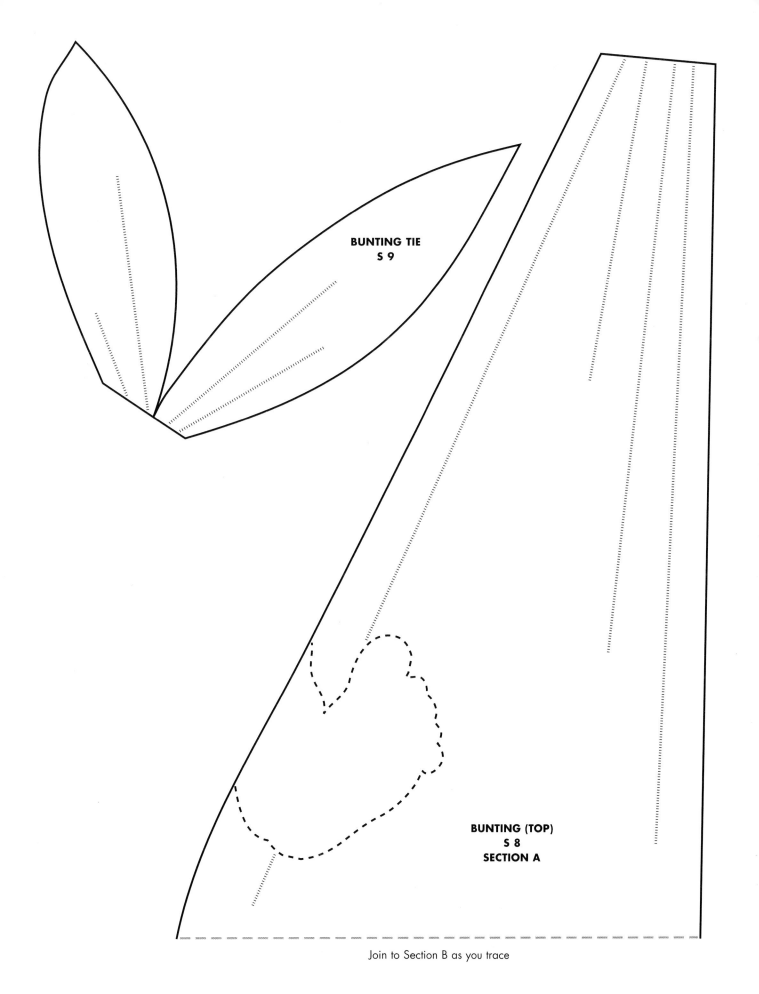

BUNTING TIE
S 9

BUNTING (TOP)
S 8
SECTION A

Join to Section B as you trace

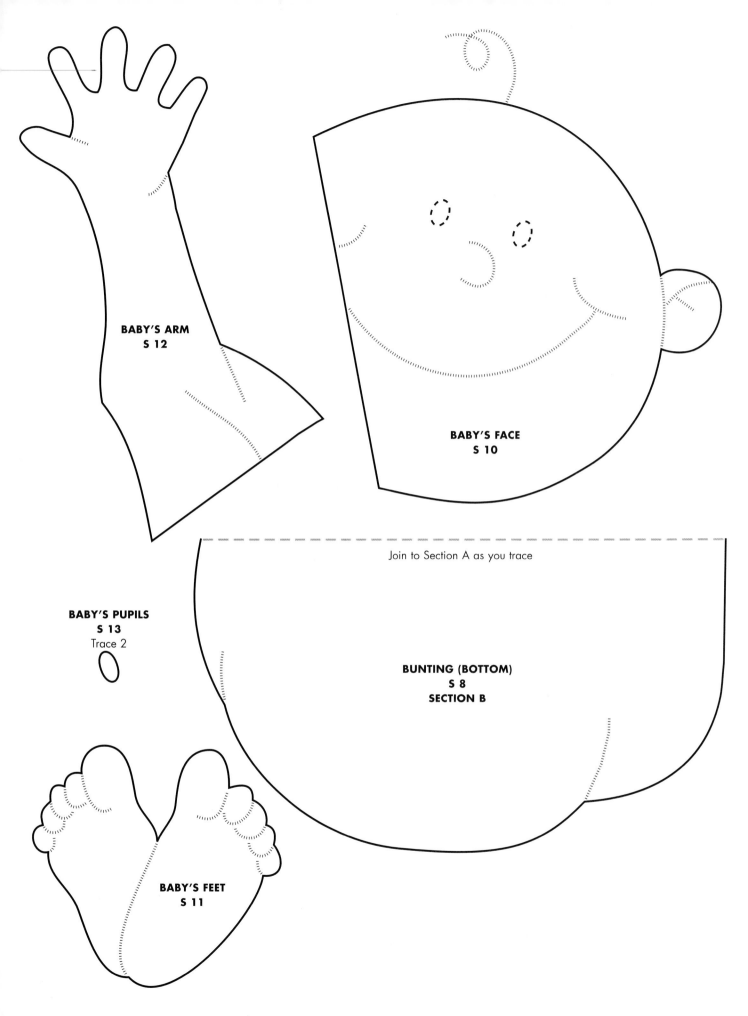

BABY'S ARM
S 12

BABY'S FACE
S 10

Join to Section A as you trace

BABY'S PUPILS
S 13
Trace 2

BUNTING (BOTTOM)
S 8
SECTION B

BABY'S FEET
S 11

LETTERS
S 20

Trace 1

Trace 1

Trace 3

Trace 2

Trace 1

Trace 1

Trace 1

Trace 1

Trace 1

Trace 1

Trace 1

TWILIGHT BLOSSOMS
PROJECT ON PAGE 37

VINE T 1 SECTION A

Join to Section B
as you trace

Use this line as a guide

STAR
T 5
Trace 2

STAR
T 5R
Trace 2

STAR
T 6
Trace 2

STAR
T 6R
Trace 2

STAR
T 4

CENTER

Join to Section C as you trace

VINE T 1 SECTION B

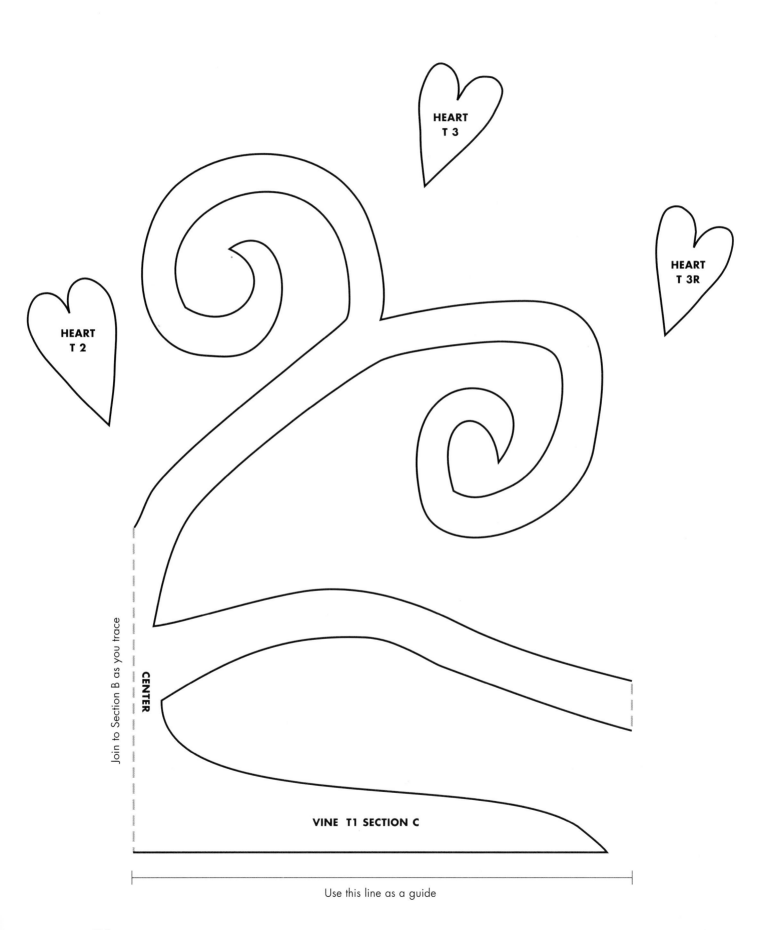

HEART
T 3

HEART
T 3R

HEART
T 2

Join to Section B as you trace

CENTER

VINE T1 SECTION C

Use this line as a guide

BLOSSOM T 7

BLOSSOM T 7R

BLOSSOM T 8

BLOSSOM T 8R

BLOSSOM T 9

BLOSSOM T 9R

VINE T 1 SECTION D

Join to Section C as you trace

**BACKGROUND PATTERN
SECTION A**

¼" seam allowance

Join to Section B as you trace

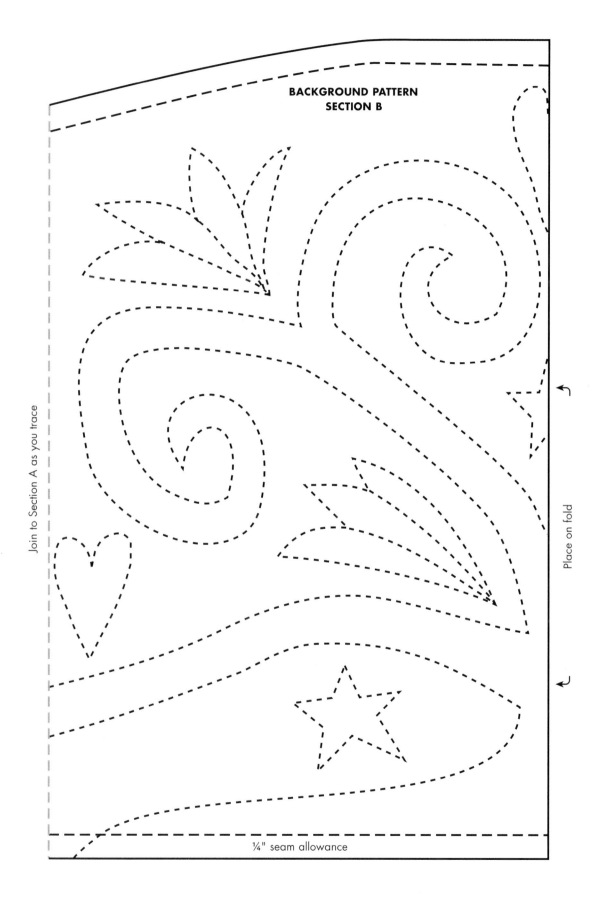

**BACKGROUND PATTERN
SECTION B**

Join to Section A as you trace

Place on fold

¼" seam allowance

A PERFECT SETTING
PROJECT ON PAGE 39

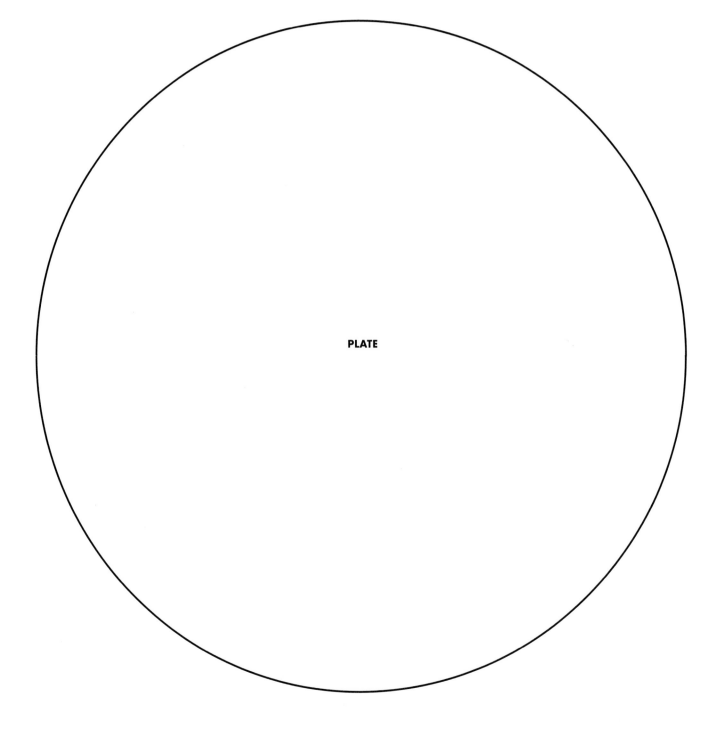

PLATE

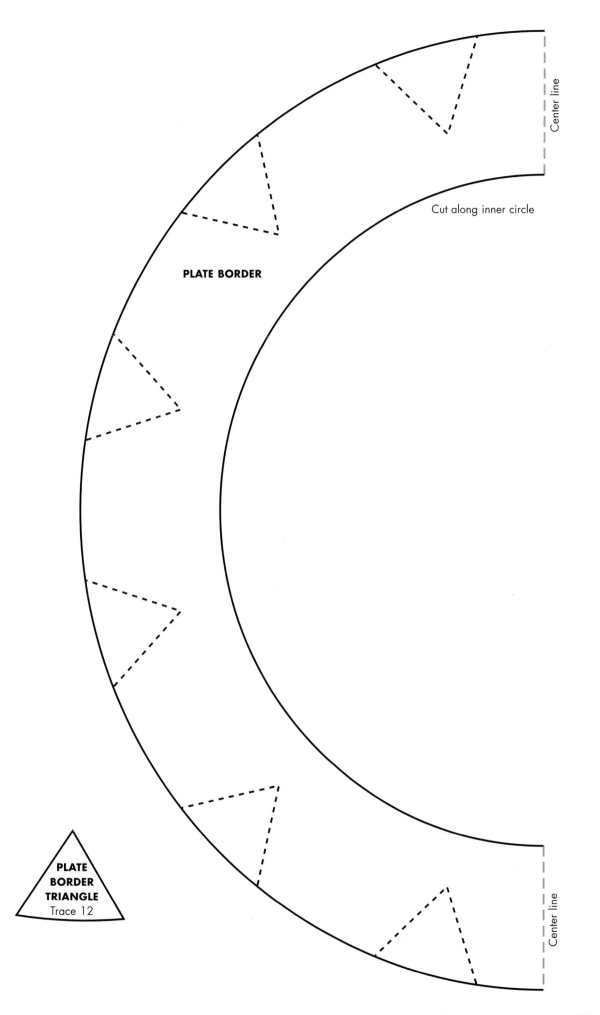

Cut along inner circle

PLATE BORDER

**PLATE
BORDER
TRIANGLE**
Trace 12

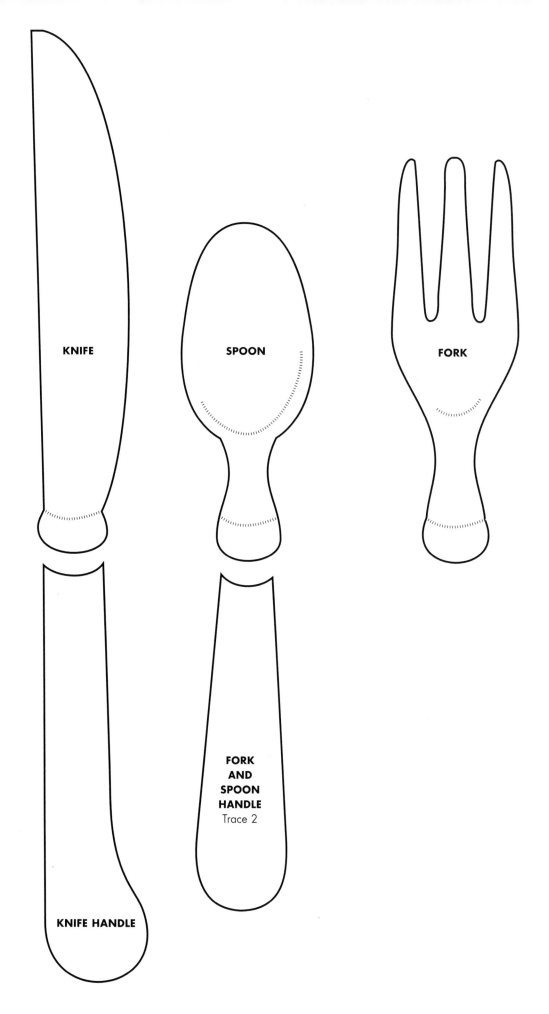

KNIFE

SPOON

FORK

FORK
AND
SPOON
HANDLE
Trace 2

KNIFE HANDLE

PUMPKIN PARTY

PROJECT ON PAGE 41

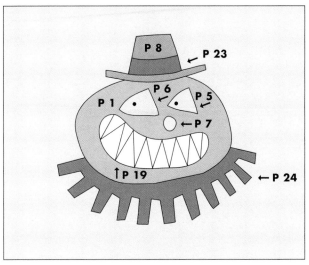

TOP PUMPKIN BLOCK

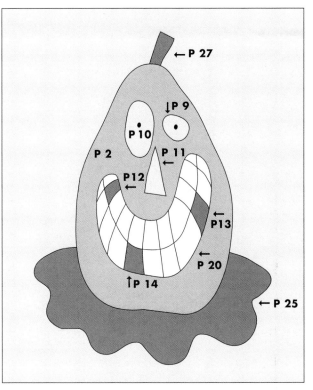

CENTER PUMPKIN BLOCK

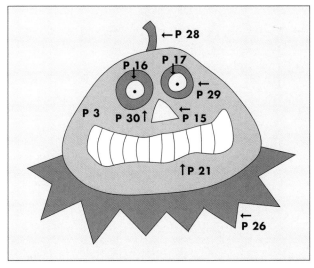

BOTTOM PUMPKIN BLOCK

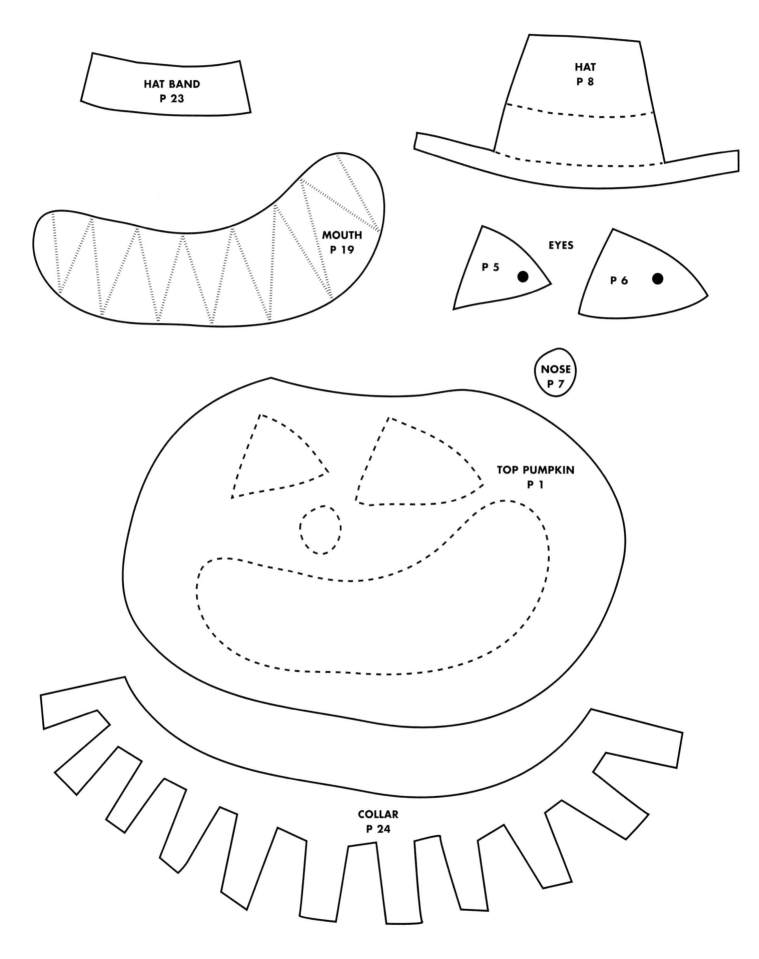

HAT BAND
P 23

HAT
P 8

MOUTH
P 19

EYES

P 5

P 6

NOSE
P 7

TOP PUMPKIN
P 1

COLLAR
P 24

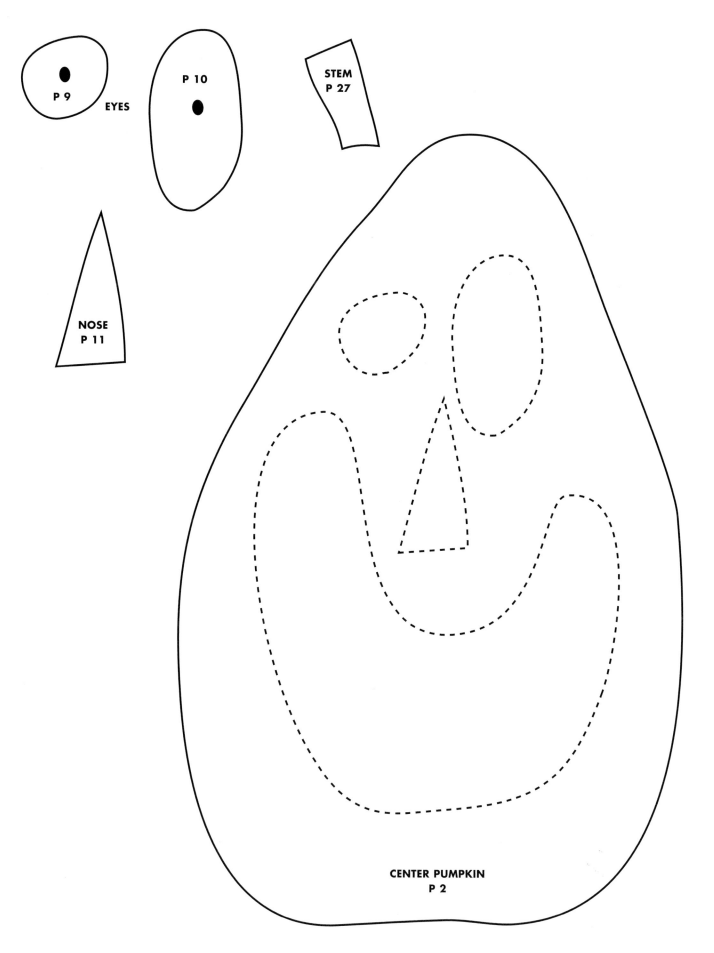

P 9

EYES

P 10

STEM
P 27

NOSE
P 11

CENTER PUMPKIN
P 2

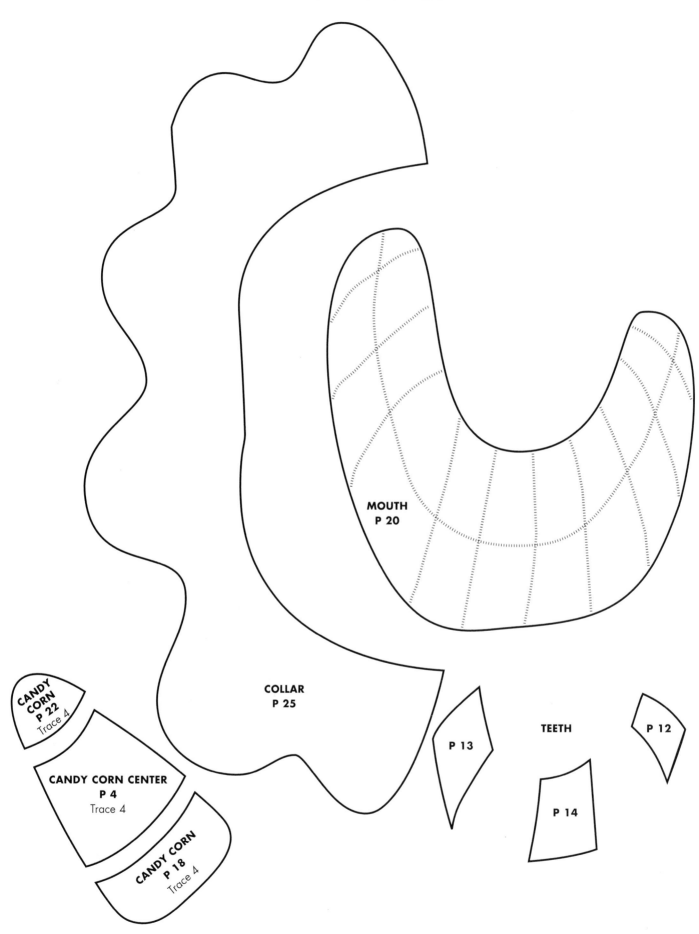

MOUTH
P 20

CANDY
CORN
P 22
Trace 4

CANDY CORN CENTER
P 4
Trace 4

CANDY CORN
P 18
Trace 4

COLLAR
P 25

P 13

TEETH

P 12

P 14

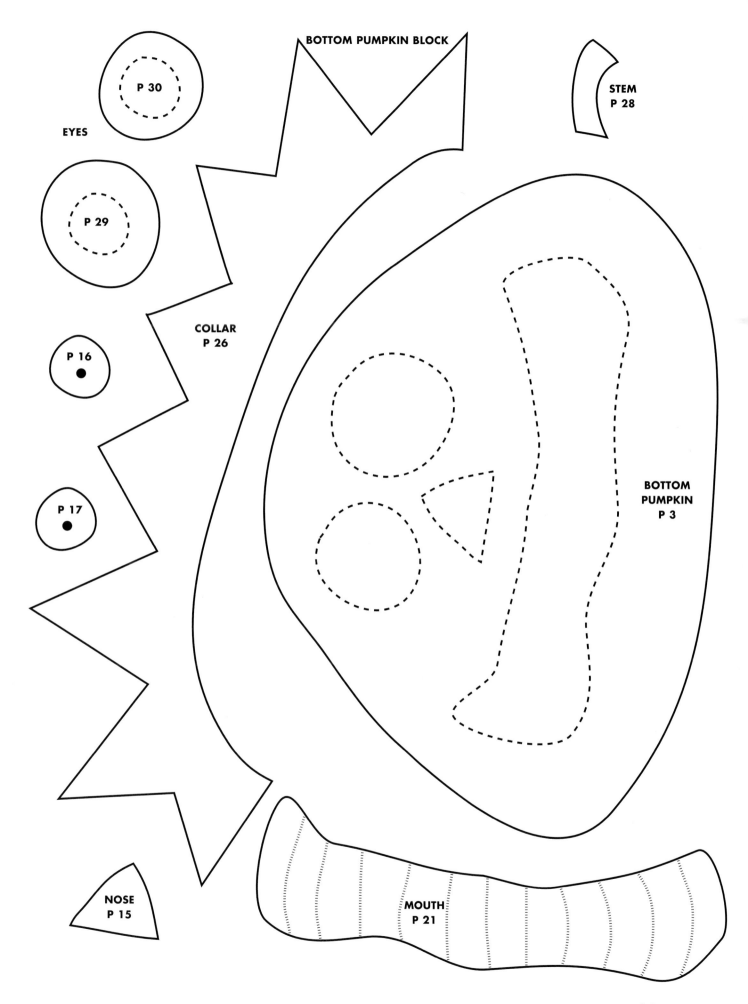

EYES

P 30

P 29

BOTTOM PUMPKIN BLOCK

STEM
P 28

COLLAR
P 26

P 16

P 17

BOTTOM
PUMPKIN
P 3

NOSE
P 15

MOUTH
P 21

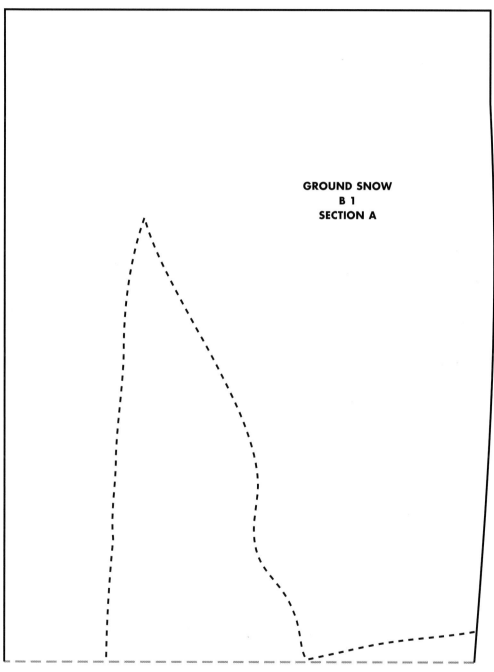

**GROUND SNOW
B 1
SECTION A**

Join to Section B as you trace

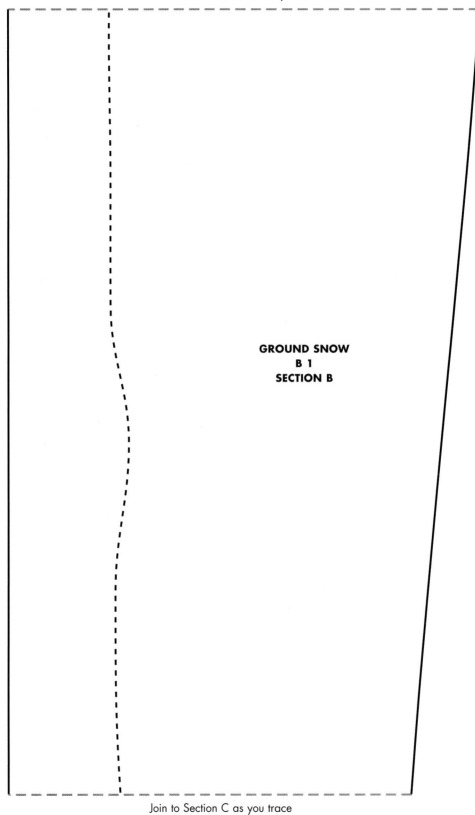

Join to Section A as you trace

GROUND SNOW
B 1
SECTION B

Join to Section C as you trace

Join to Section B as you trace

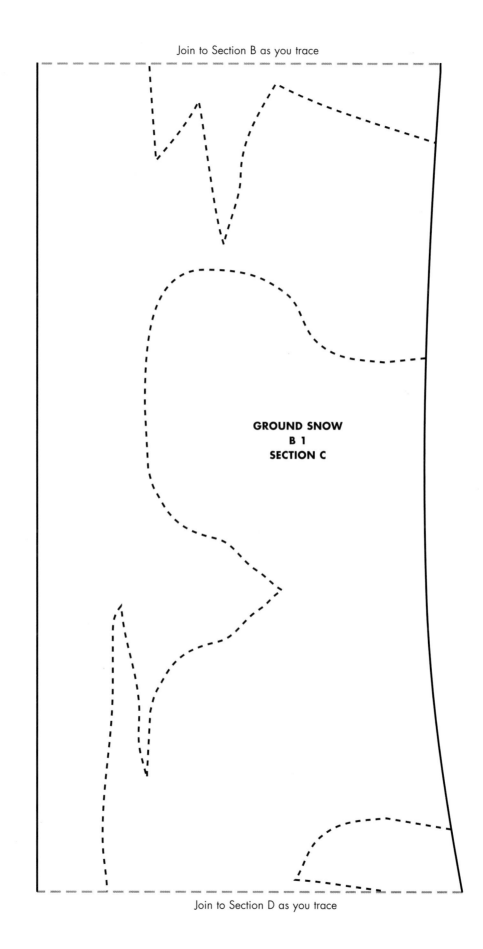

**GROUND SNOW
B 1
SECTION C**

Join to Section D as you trace

Join to Section C as you trace

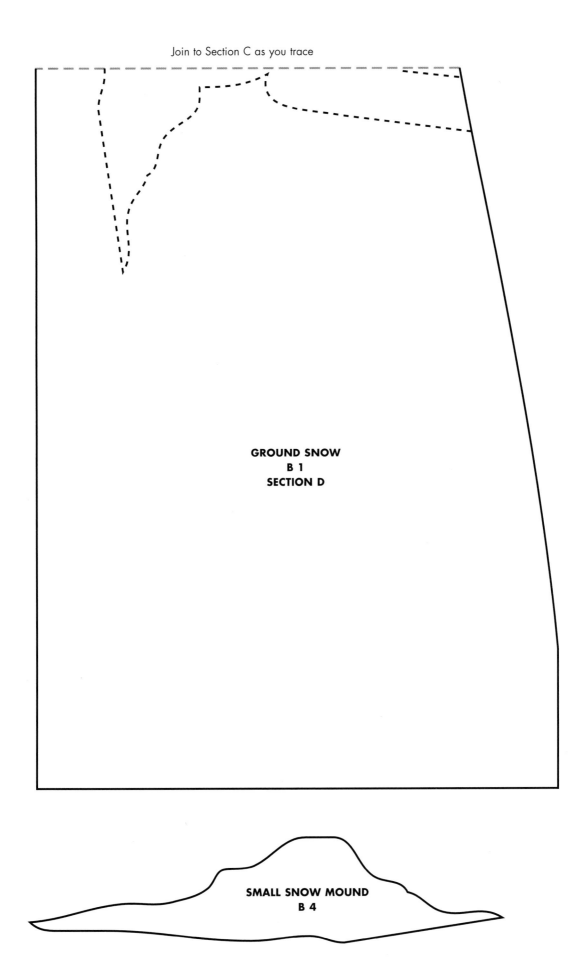

GROUND SNOW
B 1
SECTION D

SMALL SNOW MOUND
B 4

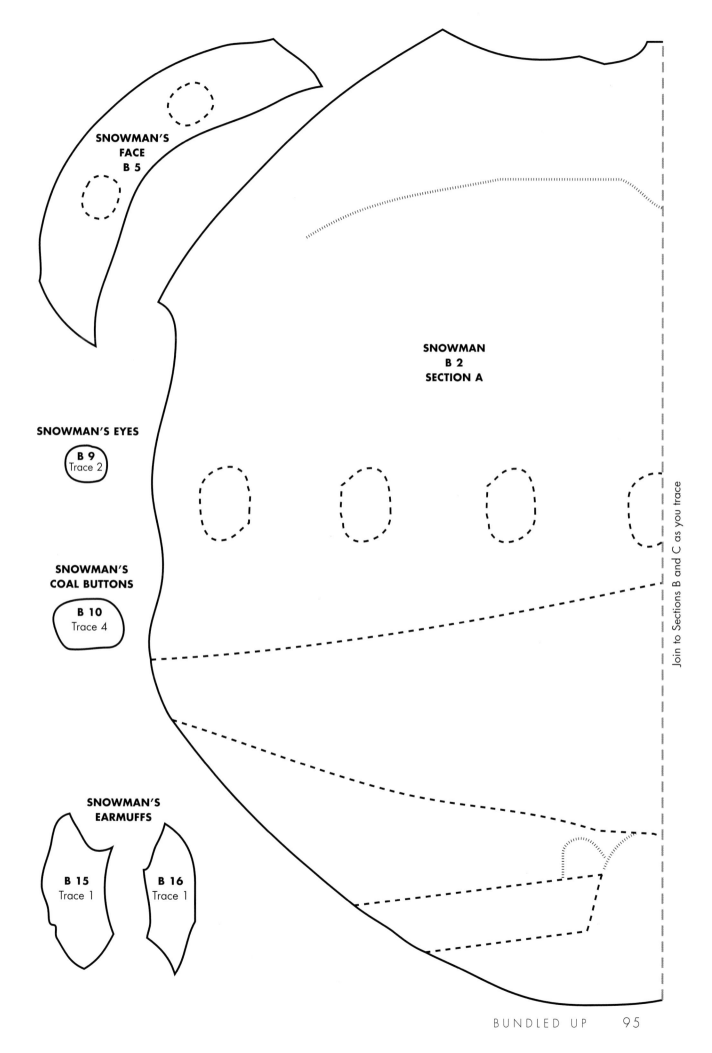

SNOWMAN'S
FACE
B 5

SNOWMAN
B 2
SECTION A

SNOWMAN'S EYES

B 9
Trace 2

SNOWMAN'S
COAL BUTTONS

B 10
Trace 4

SNOWMAN'S
EARMUFFS

B 15
Trace 1

B 16
Trace 1

Join to Sections B and C as you trace

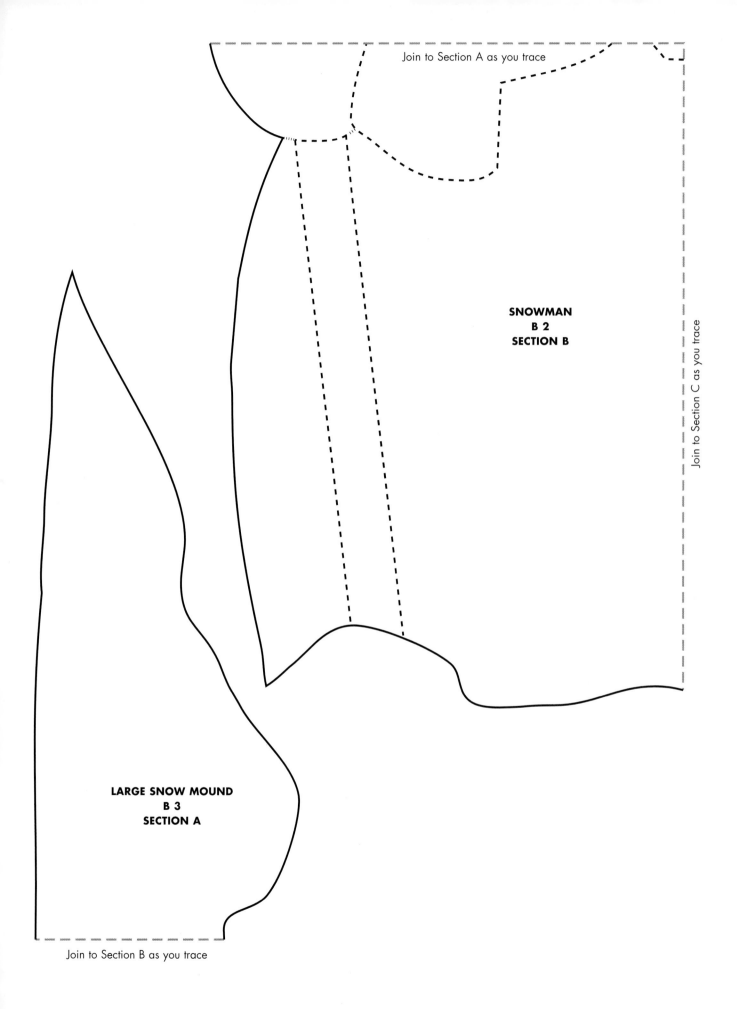

Join to Section A as you trace

SNOWMAN
B 2
SECTION B

Join to Section C as you trace

LARGE SNOW MOUND
B 3
SECTION A

Join to Section B as you trace

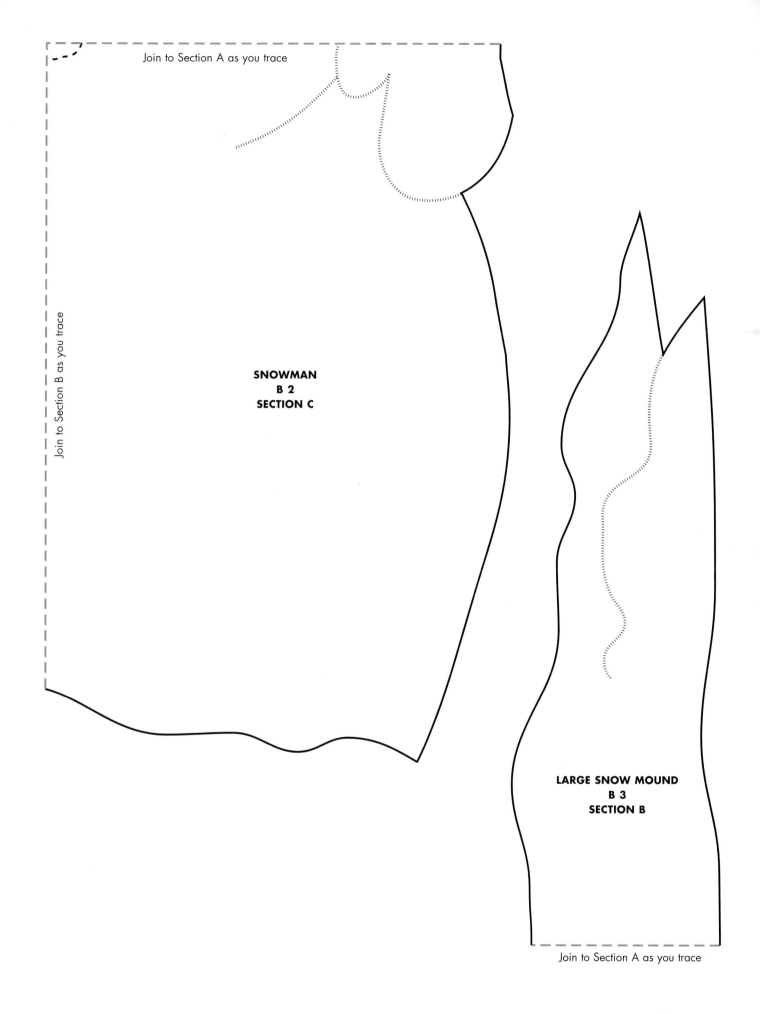

Join to Section A as you trace

Join to Section B as you trace

**SNOWMAN
B 2
SECTION C**

**LARGE SNOW MOUND
B 3
SECTION B**

Join to Section A as you trace

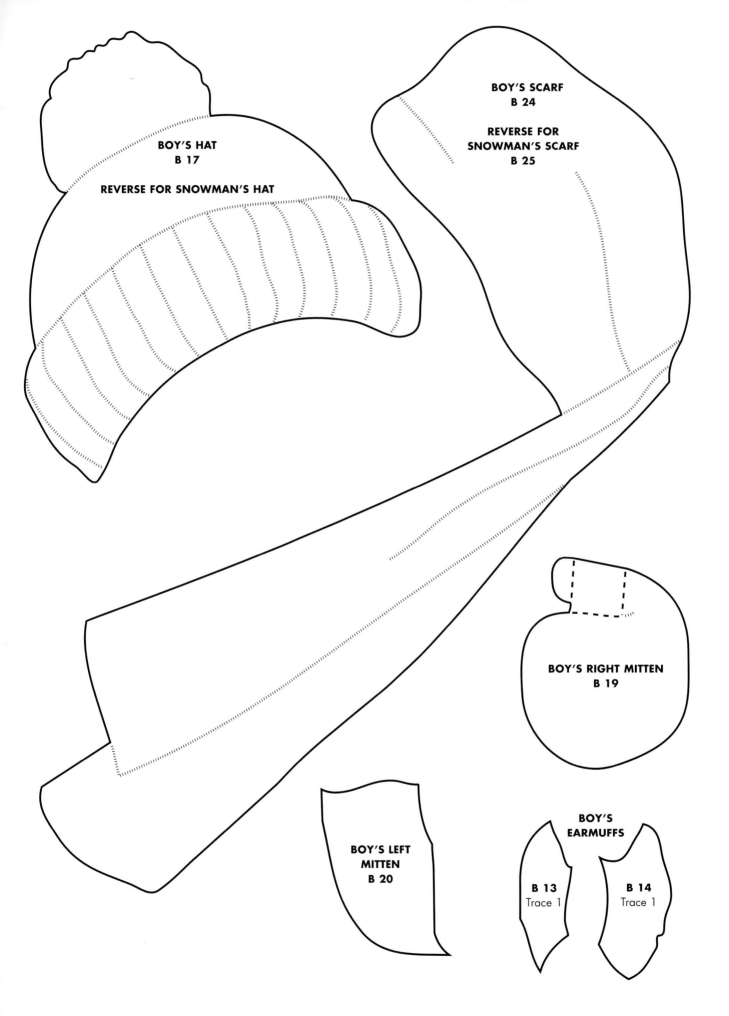

BOY'S HAT
B 17

REVERSE FOR SNOWMAN'S HAT

BOY'S SCARF
B 24

REVERSE FOR
SNOWMAN'S SCARF
B 25

BOY'S RIGHT MITTEN
B 19

BOY'S
EARMUFFS

BOY'S LEFT
MITTEN
B 20

B 13
Trace 1

B 14
Trace 1

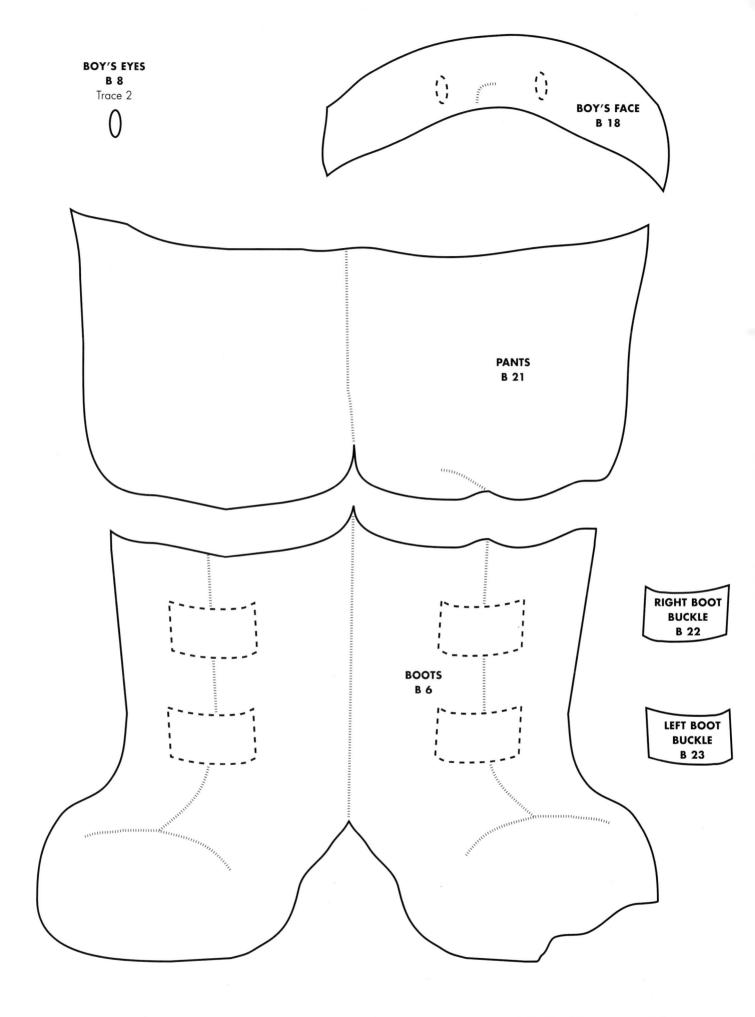

BOY'S EYES
B 8
Trace 2

BOY'S FACE
B 18

PANTS
B 21

RIGHT BOOT
BUCKLE
B 22

BOOTS
B 6

LEFT BOOT
BUCKLE
B 23

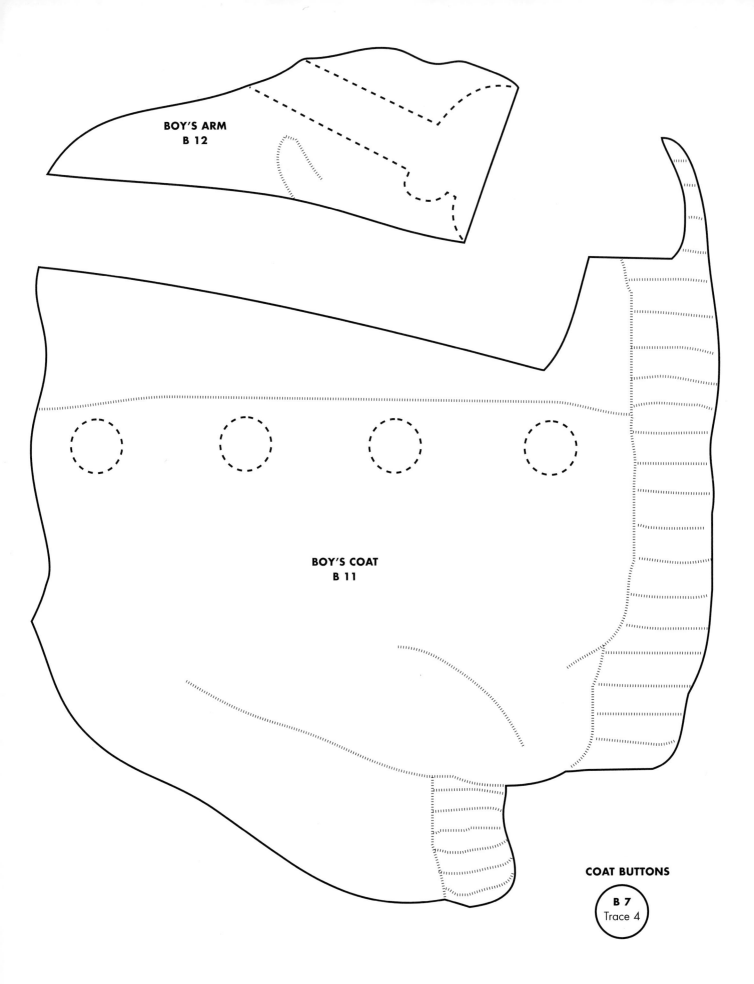

BOY'S ARM
B 12

BOY'S COAT
B 11

COAT BUTTONS

B 7
Trace 4

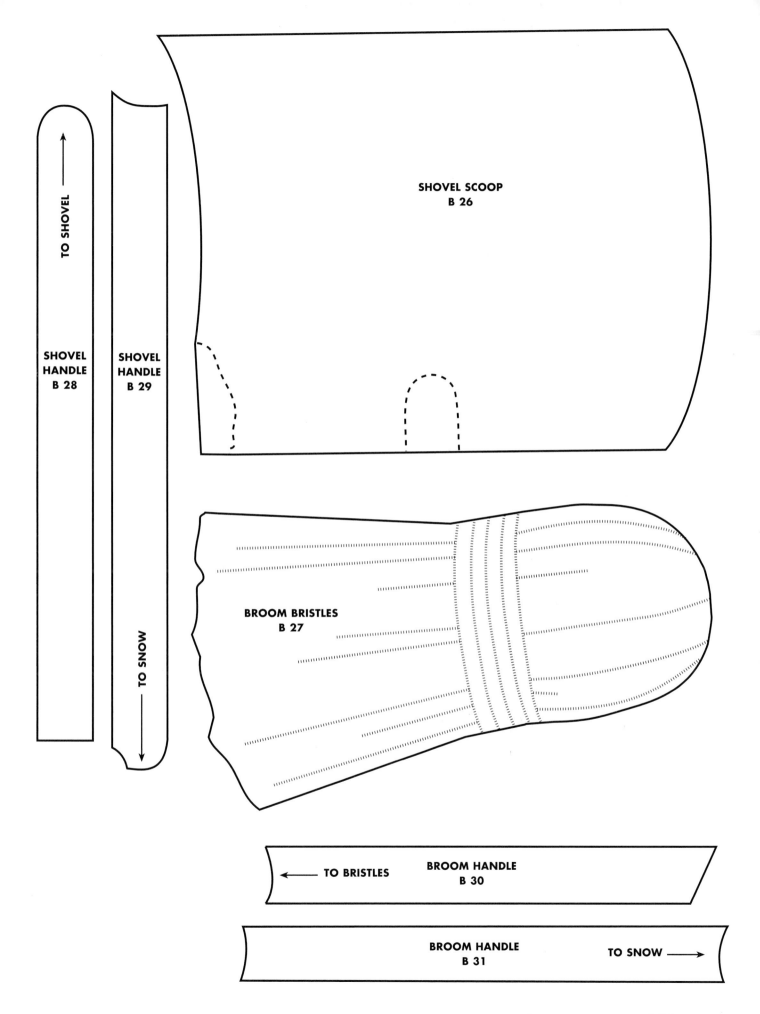

TO SHOVEL

SHOVEL
HANDLE
B 28

SHOVEL
HANDLE
B 29

TO SNOW

SHOVEL SCOOP
B 26

BROOM BRISTLES
B 27

TO BRISTLES   BROOM HANDLE
B 30

BROOM HANDLE
B 31   TO SNOW

ABOUT THE FABRIC

Following is a color key that identifies the equivalent *Marble Mania* fabric color names with the generic color names used in the projects. The first column is the generic color names; the second column is the *Marble Mania* color names. For more information on all 60 fabrics available from my *Marble Mania* line, contact Hi-Fashion Fabrics/Timeless Treasures at (212) 226-1400.

Generic color used in this book	Marble Mania color name	Generic color used in this book	Marble Mania color name
aqua	aqua	light blue	robin's egg
avocado green	avocado	light gray	silver
black	black	light orange	pumpkin
blue	cobalt	light pink	bubble gum
brown	brown	light red	tomato
buff	flesh	light yellow	merangue
burnt orange	persimmon	lime green	lime
butterscotch	butterscotch	medium blue	sky
deep blue	royal	medium green	grass
deep blue/gray	slate	mint green	mint
deep green	jade	olive green	olive
deep purple	blue	orange	orange
deep yellow	mango	orange-red	red
fuchsia	pink	powder blue	powder
gold	gold	purple	grape
golden yellow	yellow	red	cherry
gray	smoke	turquoise	turquoise
green	green	violet	violet
lavender	lavender	yellow	lemon

If you can't find my fabrics at your favorite quilt shop, contact **Hi-Fashion Fabrics/Timeless Treasures at (212) 226-1400**, or you can write to:

Out On A Whim
P.O. Box 400
Van Meter, IA 50261
e-mail: PLose@aol.com
Be sure to check out our website at http://www.patricklose.com
Please include your telephone number with any correspondence.

ABOUT THE AUTHOR

Patrick Lose has spent his professional years in a variety of creative fields. He began his career as an actor and singer, which eventually led him to designing costumes for stage and screen. Costume credits include more than 50 productions and work with celebrities such as Liza Minnelli and Jane Seymour.

An artist and illustrator since childhood, Patrick works in many mediums. When he sits down to "doodle" at the drawing board, he never knows what one of his designs might become. Whether it's designing fabric for his collections with Timeless Treasures or working on designs for quilts, wearable art, cross-stitch, greeting cards, Christmas ornaments, or home decor, he enjoys creating it all.

His crafts, clothing, and home decorating accessories have appeared frequently in many well-known magazines including *American Patchwork and Quilting*, *Better Homes & Gardens*, *Country Crafts*, *Christmas Ideas*, *Halloween Tricks and Treats*, *Folk Art Christmas*, *Santa Claus*, *Decorative Woodcrafts*, and *Craft and Wear*. Publications featuring his designs have reached over 18 million subscribers. Patrick currently lives in the quiet town of Van Meter, Iowa, just outside Des Moines.

OTHER FINE BOOKS

FROM C&T PUBLISHING:

An Amish Adventure: 2nd Edition, Roberta Horton
Anatomy of a Doll: The Fabric Sculptor's Handbook,
  Susanna Oroyan
Appliqué 12 Easy Ways! Elly Sienkiewicz
Art & Inspirations: Ruth B. McDowell, Ruth B. McDowell
The Art of Silk Ribbon Embroidery, Judith Baker Montano
The Artful Ribbon, Candace Kling
Beyond the Horizon: Small Landscape Appliqué, Valerie Hearder
Buttonhole Stitch Appliqué, Jean Wells
A Colorful Book, Yvonne Porcella
Colors Changing Hue, Yvonne Porcella
Crazy Quilt Handbook, Judith Montano
Crazy with Cotton, Diana Leone
Curves in Motion: Quilt Designs & Techniques, Judy B. Dales
Deidre Scherer: Work in Fabric & Thread, Deidre Scherer
Designing the Doll: From Concept to Construction,
  Susanna Oroyan
Dimensional Appliqué: Baskets, Blooms & Baltimore Borders,
  Elly Sienkiewicz
Easy Pieces: Creative Color Play with Two Simple Blocks, Margaret
  Miller
*Elegant Stitches: An Illustrated Stitch Guide & Source Book of
  Inspiration*, Judith Baker Montano
Everything Flowers: Quilts from the Garden, Jean and Valori Wells
Exploring Machine Trapunto, New Dimensions, Hari Walner
The Fabric Makes the Quilt, Roberta Horton
Faces & Places: Images in Appliqué, Charlotte Warr Andersen
Fantastic Figures: Ideas & Techniques Using the New Clays,
  Susanna Oroyan
Focus on Features: Life-like Portrayals in Appliqué,
  Charlotte Warr Andersen
Forever Yours, Wedding Quilts, Clothing & Keepsakes,
  Amy Barickman
Free Stuff for Quilters on the Internet, Judy Heim and
  Gloria Hansen
From Fiber to Fabric: The Essential Guide to Quiltmaking Textiles,
  Harriet Hargrave
Hand Quilting with Alex Anderson: Six Projects for Hand Quilters,
  Alex Anderson
Heirloom Machine Quilting, Third Edition, Harriet Hargrave
Imagery on Fabric, Second Edition, Jean Ray Laury
Impressionist Quilts, Gai Perry
Jacobean Rhapsodies: Composing with 28 Appliqué Designs,
  Patricia B. Campbell and Mimi Ayars
Judith Baker Montano: Art & Inspirations, Judith Baker Montano
Kaleidoscopes: Wonders of Wonder, Cozy Baker
Kaleidoscopes & Quilts, Paula Nadelstern
Make Any Block Any Size, Joen Wolfrom
Mastering Machine Appliqué, Harriet Hargrave
Michael James: Art & Inspirations, Michael James
The New Sampler Quilt, Diana Leone
On the Surface: Thread Embellishment & Fabric Manipulation,
  Wendy Hill
Papercuts and Plenty, Vol. III of Baltimore Beauties and Beyond,
  Elly Sienkiewicz

Patchwork Persuasion: Fascinating Quilts from Traditional Designs,
  Joen Wolfrom
Patchwork Quilts Made Easy, Jean Wells (co-published with
  Rodale Press, Inc.)
The Photo Transfer Handbook: Snap It, Print It, Stitch It!,
  Jean Ray Laury
Pieced Clothing Variations, Yvonne Porcella
Piecing: Expanding the Basics, Ruth B. McDowell
Plaids & Stripes: The Use of Directional Fabrics in Quilts,
  Roberta Horton
Quilts for Fabric Lovers, Alex Anderson
*Quilts from the Civil War: Nine Projects, Historical Notes, Diary
  Entries*, Barbara Brackman
Quilts, Quilts, and More Quilts! Diana McClun and Laura
  Nownes
RIVA: If Ya Wanna Look Good Honey, Your Feet Gotta Hurt…,
  Ruth Reynolds
Rotary Cutting with Alex Anderson: Tips, Techniques, and Projects,
  Alex Anderson
Say It with Quilts, Diana McClun and Laura Nownes
Scrap Quilts: The Art of Making Do, Roberta Horton
Simply Stars: Quilts that Sparkle, Alex Anderson
Six Color World: Color, Cloth, Quilts & Wearables, Yvonne Porcella
Small Scale Quiltmaking: Precision, Proportion, and Detail,
  Sally Collins
Soft-Edge Piecing, Jinny Beyer
*Start Quilting with Alex Anderson: Six Projects for First-Time
  Quilters*, Alex Anderson
Stripes in Quilts, Mary Mashuta
Through the Garden Gate: Quilters and Their Gardens, Jean and
  Valori Wells
Tradition with a Twist: Variations on Your Favorite Quilts,
  Blanche Young and Dalene Young Stone
Trapunto by Machine, Hari Walner
Wildflowers: Designs for Appliqué & Quilting, Carol Armstrong
Willowood: Further Adventures in Buttonhole Stitch Appliqué,
  Jean Wells
Yvonne Porcella: Art & Inspirations, Yvonne Porcella

**For more information,
contact us for a free catalog:**
C&T Publishing, Inc.
P.O. Box 1456
Lafayette, CA 94549
(800) 284-1114
http://www.ctpub.com
e-mail: ctinfo@ctpub.com

For quilting supplies:
Cotton Patch Mail Order
3405 Hall Lane, Dept. CTB
Lafayette, CA 94549
e-mail: cottonpa@aol.com
(800) 835-4418
(925) 283-7883